THE
ULTIMATE
BOOK OF BUSINESS
BRANDS

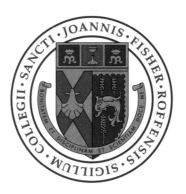

THE ULTIMATE BOOK OF BUSINESS BRANDS

INSIGHTS FROM THE WORLD'S 50 GREATEST BRANDS

DES DEARLOVE & STUART CRAINER

CAPSTONE

Copyright © Des Dearlove and Stuart Crainer 1999

The right of Des Dearlove and Stuart Crainer to be identified as the authors of
this work has been asserted in accordance with the Copyright, Designs and
Patents Act 1988

First published 1999 by

Capstone US	Capstone Publishing Limited
Business Books Network	Oxford Centre for Innovation
163 Central Avenue	Mill Street
Suite 2	Oxford OX2 0JX
Hopkins Professional Building	United Kingdom
Dover	http://www.capstone.co.uk
NH 03820	
USA	

British Library Cataloguing in Publication Data
A CIP catalogue record for this book is available from the British Library

ISBN 1-84112-016-2

Typeset in 11/14 pt Plantin by
Sparks Computer Solutions, Oxford
http://www.sparks.co.uk
Printed and bound by
T.J. International Ltd, Padstow, Cornwall

This book is printed on acid-free paper

Substantial discounts on bulk quantities of Capstone books are available to
corporations, professional associations and other organizations. If you are
in the USA or Canada, phone the LPC Group for details on (1-800-626-
4330) or fax (1-800-243-0138). Everywhere else, phone Capstone Publishing on (+44-1865-798623) or fax (+44-1865-240941).

Contents

*A*cknowledgments

W|e would like to thank many of the usual suspects who provide us with work, inspiration and lunch. At Capstone, they are Mark Allin, Richard Burton and Catherine Meyrick.

Research for this book was carried out by Stephen Coomber.

Introduction

B rands are an ever-present part of our lives – from the clothes we wear to the food we eat; from the toys our children play with to the drinks we consume; from our mobile phones to our cigarettes. We read about brands in our carefully branded newspapers. We are loyal to brands and almost everything appears to be capable of being branded – from eggs to countries. The potential for branding appears limitless. And the effort is sometimes worth it – "It's just like Pepsi Cola!" noted Russian politician Eduard Shevardnadze at the opening of the new Coca-Cola bottling plant in Tblisi, Georgia.

There is no escape. Brands have been called "the shimmering symbols of the modern age" by no less than the *Financial Times*. Not only has the world of brands expanded to take in virtually everything that can be made, provided or breathed, it has re-invented traditional relationships. Small, locally available products, have been converted into nationally and internationally renowned money-earners. A staggering 150 million Unilever products are sold every single day; over 1.2 billion people use a Gillette product every day; and 38 million people will eat at a McDonald's restaurant today.

Brands are powerful weapons. They can change the entire landscape of industries. Some even force themselves deep into the psyche of entire nations. Vegemite is an Australian cultural icon, as essential to the rearing of young Australians as their mother's milk. The Italian love-affair with Nutella is a similarly curious phenomenon – and one likely to keep psychologists at work for many years to come. The tasty chocolate spread has been celebrated for its cultural impact by Umberto Eco and, in a survey of the sexual fantasies of young Italians, was mentioned repeatedly. Nutella's maker, Ferrero, enigmatically describes its product as "the physical sublimation of chocolate."

Whether they are chocolate spread, cigarettes, cars, stores or clothes, brands are among the great icons of the twentieth century. (Why else would the great iconographer, Andy Warhol, be producing images of tins of Campbell's soup?) The fact that most of the iconic brands are American owes a great deal to the fact that American businesses have continually developed brands at a faster pace than their European counterparts. This can partly be attributed to geography. American companies had (and have) a huge, relatively homogenous national market; Europe does not. While American companies could launch massive advertising and marketing campaigns across the US and the English-speaking world, European companies learned to adapt (or not) to the cultural nuances of individual countries.

And, to a significant extent, the history of brands is tied up with the history of the USA. Trailers once travelled the American countryside laden with every possible known cure, stimulant, medicine or treatment. The medicine jamborees may have had an indifferent medical record, but their contribution to the success of brands cannot be overlooked. They played a small but significant part in the development of national branding during the late nineteenth century. Patent medicines and tobacco set the trend. Though distributed only regionally, they developed recognizable brand names and identities.

The increase of brands on a regional basis provided the foundation for growth on a much greater scale. Instead of being restricted to low-quality, regionally distributed products, brands took the great leap forward into the high quality mass market. The conditions were fertile. Efficient pan-American transportation emerged so that a successful product in Chicago could be sold in St Louis cost-effectively.

But improvements weren't limited to transport – production processes and packaging improved and advertising became almost respectable. There were also changes in trademark laws and increasing industrialization and urbanization. While the brands expanded, their management remained resolutely set in its ways. Company owners and directors took responsibility. The array of tools at their disposal – from premiums and free samples, to mass advertising – grew quickly.

The period after World War I cemented the place of brands. Advertising became increasingly prevalent and the acquisition of brands became identified with success and development. Consumers wanted Fords not motor cars; they bought from Sears rather than elsewhere.

Success brought complexity. Companies began to own a number of brands, which they were able to produce, distribute and sell *en masse*. Complexity encouraged the functional division of labor, through production lines with workers performing repetitive tasks on a mammoth scale, and the functional division of management. Management became separated into different functions such as marketing, sales, R&D and production. The separation was ruthlessly enforced. "It is not necessary for any one department to know what any other department is doing," Henry Ford propounded. "It is the business of those who plan the entire work to see that all of the departments are working … towards the same end." Ford believed that managers should work in isolation, unencumbered by the problems of their colleagues, simply concentrating on what they were employed to do.

The downside of such scientific management is now well known and accepted. Ruthlessly satirized by Charlie Chaplin in *Modern Times*, such science brought with it worker alienation, a lack of co-ordination between different functions and a complete absence of flexibility. Any sense of individual responsibility was sucked away by the system. Imaginations were never stretched; intelligence was not developed.

While scientific management took management up a lengthy blind alley, brands developed in a new direction. The great proponent of functionalized mass production, Henry Ford, fell from a position of almost total domination, thanks to the more innovative management of brands at General Motors.

In 1920 Ford was making a car a minute and the famously black Model T accounted for 60 percent of the market. General Motors managed to scrimp and scrape its way to around 12 percent. With Ford cornering the mass market, the accepted wisdom was that the only alternative for competitors lay in the negligibly sized luxury market. GM chief Alfred P. Sloan thought otherwise and concentrated GM's attentions on the, as yet non-existent, middle market. His aim was a car for "every purse and every purpose."

At the time, GM was an unwieldy combination of companies with eight models that basically competed against each other as well as against Ford. Sloan cut the eight models down to five and decided that rather than competing with each other, each model – an individual brand – would be targeted at a particular segment of the market. The five GM brands – the Chevrolet, Oldsmobile, Pontiac, Buick and Cadillac – were to be updated and changed regularly and came in more than one color. Ford continued to offer functional, reliable cars; GM offered choice. By 1925, with its new organization and commitment to annual changes in its models, GM had overtaken Ford, which continued to persist with its faithful old Model T. GM made brands work. "Back then, if you said the word Pontiac, any consumer in the country could tell you what kind of person drove it," said *Business Week*.[1]

While Sloan at GM proved the importance of brands, in 1931 Procter & Gamble took functional organization a stage further when it created a new function: brand management. With brands like Ivory and Camay bath soaps, P&G believed that the best way to organize itself would be to give responsibility to a single individual: a brand manager. (And you can't argue with P&G's development since. Its revenues now near $40 billion.)

The system did not transform the world overnight, but gradually brand management became an accepted functional activity, an adjunct to sales and marketing – and often a fairly junior adjunct at that. Its popularity was fuelled by the economic boom of the 1950s, which brought a plethora of new products and brands. These were supplemented by developments such as shopping centers and the emergence of television advertising. We had never had it so good and never had so much. Brand management provided some hope of order amid the confusion introduced by prosperity.

By 1967, 84 percent of large manufacturers of consumer packaged goods manufacturers in the United States had brand managers. Though titles have changed, this system largely prevails today. It is only in the 1990s that the brand management system began to be questioned through trends such as re-engineering which sought to break down the long-established functional barriers.

Brandbite

"Well-managed brands live on, only bad brand managers die."
— *George Bull*

Defining brands

Along the way our notion of what constitutes a brand has changed – usually slowly and subtly – with the times. In the beginning came the product. Branding was a mark on the product – a signature or symbol – signifying its origin or ownership. The traditional view of what constitutes a brand is summed up by marketing guru Philip Kotler in his classic textbook, *Marketing Management*. Kotler writes: "[A brand name is] a name, term, sign, symbol or design, or a combination of these, which is intended to identify the goods or services of one group of sellers and differentiate them from those of competitors."[2]

The trouble with older definitions of brands is that they remain preoccupied with the physical product. The product stands alone; the brand exists within corporate ether. The product comes first and the brand does little more than make it clear which company made the product and where. John Pemberton's brain tonic is the product, but the brand – Coca-Cola – is much more.

A more recent definition comes from Richard Koch in his book *The Financial Times Guide to Management and Finance*. Koch defines a brand as: "A visual design and/or name that is given to a product or service by an organization in order to differentiate it from competing products and which assures consumers that the product will be of high and consistent quality." Reflecting the emphasis of our times, Koch stresses differentiation – making your product or service different (or seeming to be different) – and achieving consistent quality.

More recently, and perhaps more usefully, three American consultants have defined branding as "creating a mutually acknowledged relationship between the supplier and buyer that transcends isolated transactions or specific individuals." It is a significant sign of our times that the brand is now pinned around a "relationship" rather than a product.[3]

Perhaps the most practical and contemporary definition of brands comes from the consultants Booz-Allen & Hamilton: "Brands are a shorthand way of communicating critical data to the market to influence decisions. Across a multitude of consumer-focused industries, brands are an important means for differentiation and competitive advantage, although they are most influential when customers lack the data to make informed product choices and/or when the differentiation between competitors' versions of the same product are small to non-existent. Additionally, brands take on more significance when consumers place great importance on the decision being made."[4]

In search of the ultimate brands

In this new world filled with brands, we went in search of the ultimate brands, the physical and mental sublimation of brands. We found that that ultimate brands have a number of characteristics:

1. The ultimate brands are universal

Ultimate brands can be in unsung businesses selling mundane products in innovative ways. The modern world of brands extends to all industries, all businesses. It doesn't matter what business you are in, branding is important. Once the world of brands was dominated by fast moving consumer goods. Now it is filled with retailers – from Benetton to Wal-Mart – and financial services companies. They realize that branding can provide competitive advantage no matter whether you sell hot-dogs or provide cleaning services.

Witness the New Pig Corporation. Despite its name, New Pig has to be taken seriously. With more than 300 employees and anticipated sales of $77 million in 1998, New Pig is growing at a healthy annual rate of 10 percent. But then, you don't have to take the company that seriously. After all, its employee cafeteria is called the Pig Trough and its catalog is known to one and all as the Pigalog.

Brandbite

"Brand loyalty is very much like an onion. It has layers and a core. The core is the user who will stick with you until the very end."

– Edwin Artzt

New Pig is not a PR firm with a slick line in irony. It sells a range of 2500 cleaning, absorbent and containment products to manufacturing companies virtually all through direct mail. New Pig's products – items like absorbent socks and mats – are neither sexy nor particularly amusing. To each unheralded product, New Pig brings the Pig brand. The New Pig branding is all pervasive. There are boar facts and the catalog even features a Pork Avenue collection of Oink products, including the oinking pig hat and the oink sweatshirt. The company can be called on 800-HOT-HOGS, and its HQ is One Pork Avenue.

There is, New Pig cheerfully admits, nothing clever and strategic behind the New Pig brand. The aim is to draw people in and

---

Universal brands

- Gillette
- Heineken
- McDonald's
- Microsoft
- Virgin
- Yamaha

make dull products fun. It works. There is no doubt that branding the previously unbrandable has given the company a competitive advantage. Imitators have tried to make inroads into the market – there have been snakes and gators – but all lacked the elan of New Pig. The brand's the thing.

2. The ultimate brands are personal; psychological as well as physical

"Your T-shirt with the distinctive Champion 'C' on the sleeve, the blue jeans with the prominent Levi's rivets, the watch with the hey-this-certifies-I-made-it icon on the face, your fountain pen with the maker's symbol crafted into the end … You're branded, branded, branded," says management guru Tom Peters. The ultimate brands strike a personal chord with you. They make you feel better, different, bigger, smaller, happier, more comfortable, warmer, more confident. They reach parts other brands only dream about.

In this new era, brands are driven by consumers. They are psychological, as well as physical. Brands are about hearts and minds. "A brand is a promise, and, in the end, you have to keep your promises. A product is the artifact of the truth of a promise. Coke promises refreshment; Gateway Computer promises to be your wagon master across the Silicon prairie. There is no difference between what you sell and what you believe," says futurist Watts Wacker. Selling is believing. More importantly, people buy what they trust and believe

---

Personal brands

- Apple
- The GAP
- Harley-Davidson
- Levi-Strauss
- Marlboro
- Nike
- Virgin

in, and are prepared to pay a premium price for it. In the end, branding works because belief sells.

Branding is believing. Witness the story of Schlitz, an American beer. It is now found only occasionally among the mass of taps bearing the logos Budweiser, Miller, Molson and the like. But in 1974 Schlitz was America's second most popular brand of beer. It held 16.1 percent of the massive American market and appeared destined for a comfortable long life. Then the brewers introduced a revolutionary new process – "accelerated batch fermentation." This saved time and money. It appeared a triumph for all concerned. The beer tasted the same – what else could matter?

The trouble was that customers didn't have faith in the new process. They believed the beer was below the standard they had come to expect – it tasted the same, but customers *believed* it wasn't the same. Schlitz's market share fell to less than a single percentage mark and the value of its name declined from in excess of $1 billion in 1974 to around $75 million in 1980.

There is more. The personal nature of branding means that people are increasingly treating themselves and being treated as brands. For sports stars and actresses this has long been a fact of life. Now, however, mere mortals are using branding to develop their careers. "We are CEOs of our own companies: Me Inc. To be in business today, our most important job is to be head marketer for the brand called You," says Tom Peters. We have to market and sell ourselves like brands to progress.

Tom Peters should know because he is at the vanguard of the branding of business ideas. Management gurus are increasingly behaving like brands. Harvard Business School professor Michael Porter is a highly successful management thinker, author and consultant – he says he is aware of protecting and developing "the Michael Porter brand." He knows that if he spreads himself too thinly and attempts to do too many things, the source of his fame and renown – his intellectual rigor and insight – will wither away.

Brandbite

"I am irresistible, I say, as I put on my designer fragrance. I am a merchant banker, I say, as I climb out of my BMW: I am a juvenile lout, I say, as I down a glass of extra strong lager. I am handsome, I say, as I don my Levi's jeans."

— John Kay

---

3. The ultimate brands have the power to re-invent businesses and, sometimes, entire industries

Witness the phenomenal success of Absolut vodka, which has emerged from nowhere as the vodka brand of our day. It is now the number one imported vodka in the US with 60 percent of the market. Absolut's success has been built on brilliant brand development. A clever ad campaign has established Absolut as a brand for its times. Ironic and sophisticated, the ads (developed by TBWA Chiat/Day) with their variations on the Absolut bottle, have become classics – so much so that a book of the ads sold a staggering 150,000 copies.

The most surprising thing about Absolut is that it is produced by a state-owned industry. Owned by the Swedish state, Absolut is probably the best possible advertisement for state control. Indeed, in these privatized times Absolut is increasingly the only ad for successful state control. Absolut is also testament to how powerful branding can be. Ten years ago, the brand was virtually unknown; its product unfashionable; its market dominated by long-established brands. Smirnoff ruled the roost. No more.

Witness the National Basketball Association. In 1996, the NBA amassed $1.2 billion from ticket sales and television rights. Ten years previously, the figure was $255 million. Promotions, sponsorships and an array of commercial links brought in $3 billion (against $107 million in 1986).

What is interesting about this is that the actual product is very limited. The NBA has a mere 29 teams. Nor is basketball a univer-

---

Power brands

- American Express
- Benetton
- Disney
- Federal Express
- General Electric
- Häagen-Dazs
- Holiday Inn
- Ikea

- McDonald's
- McKinsey & Co.
- Nike
- Sears, Roebuck
- Starbucks
- Swatch
- Wal-Mart

---

sally popular sport. Name a British basketball team or player? Yet, the NBA has succeeded because of its expertise in brand development.

In *Radical Marketing*, Glenn Rifkin and Sam Hill identify a number of elements crucial to NBA's success. First, it has developed line extensions – such as a professional woman's league. Second, the NBA has built and nurtured a plethora of strategic alliances. It has worked closely with retailers and television networks. Third, it has gained visibility while others have footed the bill. When Michael Jordan advertises Nike, he is also advertising the NBA. And, finally, it has a happy knack of keeping its name in the news.

Behind this are a number of other important elements – an astute leader, high quality standards throughout the use of the NBA brand, motivated workers (on the court and off) and a global perspective. The question must be whether this recipe for brand success can outlast the career of the man who did much to ignite it, Michael Jordan.

4. The ultimate brands are global

Globalization is one of the great rallying cries of our times. Nowhere is it louder than in the world of brands.

Global Brands

- Barbie
- Benetton
- Budweiser
- Coca-Cola
- Disney
- General Electric
- Goodyear
- Hewlett-Packard
- Heinz
- Hertz
- IBM
- Kellogg's
- Lego
- McDonald's
- Mars
- Mercedes-Benz
- Nescafé
- Rolls-Royce
- Sony

Global brands are, of course, more easily proclaimed than achieved. Combining global and local elements is a minefield – nowhere more so than in Europe where cultural and regional differences abound. For example, research by market research company Mintel found that 22 percent of French people are likely to sample a product if it is endorsed by a celebrity. The British remain studiously unimpressed – only one percent said they would be influenced. This, of course, begs the question as to why television advertisements in the UK consistently use a host of minor celebrities.

Different angles work in different countries. The Spanish, for example, are attracted by anything to do with sport or modernity. But it is not only national tastes and preoccupations that the brand must play to. Approaches may differ according to a brand's place and standing in the marketplace in an individual country. The soft drink Orangina is positioned and priced differently in various countries. It is a global brand which is highly responsive to local markets. In France, for example, it is highly popular – the second soft drink after Coke – while in the UK it competes as a premium brand in the orange carbonated soft drink market against local brands such as Tango or Sunkist. Schweppes is used as a mixer in the UK and Ireland, but as a straight drink in France and Spain. Finding a neat approach that suits the needs of both markets is practically impossible.

From an organizational point of view, strength in a particular national market generally means that the brand is given greater independence – the local rather than global is emphasized.

5. The ultimate brands inform

At its simplest, branding is a statement of ownership. Cows are branded and, in the commercial world, branding can be traced back to trademarks placed on Greek pots in the seventh century BC and, later, to medieval tradesmen who put trademarks on their products to protect themselves and buyers against inferior imitations. (Of course, in the modern world people are adept at copying trademarks – whether they are Lacoste, Sony, Rolex or Le Coq Sportif – and producing imitations, which are often highly accurate.)

Today, brands are a ready source of information as well as identification. "The point of brands is, and always has been, to provide information. The form of that information varies from market to market, and from time to time. Some products make a visible statement about their users' style, modernity or wealth – examples include clothes, cars and accessories. Others purport to convey reliability, say, or familiarity, or something else. Whatever the

---

Informative brands

- American Express
- Holiday Inn
- Intel
- Kellogg's
- Kodak

- Mercedes-Benz
- Reuters
- Rolls-Royce
- Sony
- Toyota

information, however, the right question to ask is this: does the buyer still need or want it," acutely observed an editorial in *The Economist*.[5]

Witness the earth's biggest bookstore – with 2.5 million books – Amazon.com. It is the exemplar of electronic commerce, the first great electronic retail brand.

Back in the electronic mists, the first books ordered through Amazon were dispatched in the fall of 1994 (personally packed by founder, Jeff Bezos, and his wife); in 1997 Amazon sold its one millionth book. In 1997, sales approached $148 million, an eight-fold increase year on year. In 1998 sales grew 838 percent.

Brandbite

"Your premium brand better be delivering something special or it's not going to get the business."

– *Warren Buffett*

The original model for Amazon.com was to provide the world's largest bookshop, but it quickly found that it was actually selling information as much as books. Today, for example, Amazon ("the toast of cyberspace" according to the *Financial Times*) will send customers an e-mail every time a new book comes out on a subject in which they have registered an interest. That information also helps the company better understand its customers and target its marketing.

The site also encourages "chat" among its users as part of its service. To encourage discussion, it not only posts book reviews from leading newspapers, it also encourages customers to send in their own reviews which are published on the Amazon site. This, say McKinsey consultants John Hagel and Arthur Armstrong in their book *Net Gain*, is a powerful form of "community building" – a new trick for electronic channels – something that adds value to web transactions and builds the strength of the electronic brand.

Brandbite

"Today brands are everything, and all kinds of products and services – from accounting firms to sneaker makers to restaurants – are figuring out how to transcend the narrow boundaries of their categories and become a brand surrounded by a Tommy Hilfiger-like buzz."

– Tom Peters

6. The ultimate brands are handled with care

At one time, brands were unhappily and inaccurately associated with the hard-selling entrepreneurial superficiality of the 1980s when deals were everything and brands changed hands as readily as stolen watches in a downtown bar. Conglomerates owned portfolios of brands and managed them to maximize market share. Often, the spirit of the brand – its uniqueness – was lost in the process. There is a paradox here. The lesson that companies learned the hard way is that although brands can be cynically manipulated for profit in the short run, to remain strong over time they require periodic injections of freshness. Brands have to be reborn or they will die; change them too much and you slay the Golden Goose.

Careful brands

- General Electric
- Harvard Business School
- Hewlett-Packard
- Lego
- Levi-Strauss
- Mars
- Red Cross
- Reuters
- Rolls-Royce
- Sony
- Xerox

There can be no better or clearer example of this than the experience of New Coke. In 1985, the late Roberto Goizueta, CEO of the Coca-Cola Company, decided to do the unthinkable and change the famous Coke formula. In doing so he made the mistake of interfering with one of the most powerful brands on the planet. Consumers reacted with passion. Faced by potential catastrophe, Goizueta's solution was a superb piece of inventive rebranding: Coke Classic was born.

What the mighty Coca-Cola and others have learned the hard way is that brands are sensitive things – finely balanced between past and future. Remember Schlitz. You must change brands to keep their vitality, but change them too much and you alienate your loyal customers. There is no such thing as a bullet-proof brand. Brand management is a subtle and mysterious art.

In recent years, brands have been brought back to earth. Companies appreciate that brands are neither frivolous nor a necessary evil, but important, expensive and potentially lucrative investments. That they are all-embracing is a fact of life – caused in part by the human need for re-assurance, labeling and ease of identity.

7. Brands are simple

For all this, the function of brands is fundamentally straightforward. Brands are little more than prompts, symbols and representations – activities which have been used since we started buying and selling

---

Simple brands

- Benetton
- The GAP
- Häagen-Dazs
- Ikea
- Mars

- Nike
- Red Cross
- Starbucks
- Swatch
- Wrigley's

things. Brands are marketing shorthand which companies hope will lead us to purchase their particular products.

8. Almost anything can be branded, anything, anywhere on earth

In the age of brands, nothing is beyond branding – witness the way branding techniques are now routinely applied to football teams, pop groups, political parties and, even, countries.

A trio of management consultants, Sam Hill, Sandeep Dayal and Jack McGrath, have actually advised on how to brand sand and any other "lowly differentiated" product or service.[6]

The first step in branding, suggest Hill, Dayal and McGrath, is simply to "carve up the market from every angle – profits, needs, behaviors – to identify those customers who are responsive to differentiation." Taking as their starting point the belief that no market is completely homogeneous, they argue that customers can be divided into three groups – gold standard customers (willing to pay premium prices if their, sometimes exacting, requirements are met); potentials (more interested in price, but perspectives can be moved); and incorrigibles (short-term and price fixated).

With greater understanding of customers – there is no substitute for knowing the market – companies can move onto the second stage of branding: differentiation. This was once entirely product-related. Now, service-based differentiation is increasingly in importance. Differentiators can then be "bundled" together to make up a brand

---

'Anything' brands

- Harvard Business School
- Intel
- McKinsey & Co.
- Microsoft
- Red Cross
- Reuters
- Wrigley's

which is communicated consistently and strongly. Finally, a company must align itself "to reinforce and defend the brand and the underlying sources of differentiation." "The key is to take a disciplined, deliberate approach that begins with the market, understands how to create and deliver value and, most importantly, figures out how to get paid for it," they conclude. "Getting paid for it requires branding, extending the relationship beyond the transaction to encompass the full organization." Extending relationships lies at the heart of all of the ultimate brands.

Brandbite

"Any damn fool can put on a deal, but it takes genius, faith, and perseverance to create a brand."

– David Ogilvy

The Ultimate Book of Brands

This is not the final word on brands. Nor is it a definitive listing of the greatest 50 brands of the twentieth century or any other time scale. It is our personal choice based on our readings around the subject and canvassing of numerous experts in branding theory and best practice. The brands have been selected because of their influence and impact as much as because of any other measure. In branding, more than any other part of the business world, impact is all. We hope the 50 brands we have selected are an eclectic and interesting mix. They are brands with stories.

Happily, many of the brands we feature would be included if our selection was based on financial criteria alone.

The world's most valuable brands[7]

Brand	Brand value ($ billion)
Coca-Cola	47.99
Marlboro	47.64
IBM	23.70
McDonald's	19.94
Disney	17.07
Sony	14.46
Kodak	14.44
Intel	13.27
Gillette	11.99
Budweiser	11.99
Nike	11.13
Kellogg's	10.67
AT&T	10.39
Nescafé	10.34
GE	10.29
Hewlett-Packard	9.42
Pepsi	9.32
Microsoft	8.99
Frito-Lay	8.99
Levi's	8.17

The most potent link between these brands is that of culture. The ultimate brands stand the test of time not because of advertising spend, good PR or incessant promotions, but because of the strength of the cultures which lie behind them. In many of the ultimate brands, corporate culture has become intertwined with the brand. You can't see the join. People within the organizations are not cynical or dismissive. They believe in the brand and what it stands for. What the brand actually does or looks like may be mundane, but in the world of branding belief truly is all.

Des Dearlove & Stuart Crainer, 1999

The brands time-line

1. The originators (pre-twentieth century)
- American Express
- Budweiser
- Coca-Cola
- General Electric
- Gillette
- Goodyear
- Guinness
- Heinz
- Kodak
- Levi-Strauss
- Red Cross
- Reuters
- Sears, Roebuck

2. Pace setters (1900–1950)
- Disney
- Guinness
- Harley-Davidson
- Harvard Business School
- Heineken
- Hoover
- IBM
- Mars
- McKinsey & Co
- Mercedes
- Nescafé
- Sony
- Toyota
- Wrigley's

3. The first golden age of brands (1950s)
- Barbie
- Marlboro
- Hewlett-Packard
- Holiday Inn
- Lego
- Wal-Mart

4. The lull before the storm (1960s and 1970s)
- Apple
- Benetton
- Federal Express
- Ikea
- Intel

5. The global golden age (1980s and 1990s)
- The GAP
- Häagen-Dazs
- Microsoft
- Nike
- Starbucks

The ultimate businesses

Retailers
- Ikea
- Sears, Roebuck
- Starbucks
- Wal-Mart

Financial services
- American Express

High-tech
- Apple
- Hewlett-Packard
- IBM
- Intel
- Microsoft
- Sony

Fashion
- Benetton
- The GAP
- Levi-Strauss
- Nike

Cigarettes and alcohol
- Budweiser
- Guinness
- Heineken
- Marlboro

Food and drink
- Coca-Cola
- Häagen-Dazs
- Heinz
- Mars
- Nescafé
- Wrigley's

Leisure and entertainment
- Barbie
- Disney
- Lego
- Sony

Services
- Federal Express
- Harvard Business School
- Hertz
- Holiday Inn
- McDonald's
- McKinsey & Co
- Virgin
- Reuters

Products
- General Electric
- Gillette
- Hoover
- Kodak
- Swatch
- Xerox

Transportation
- Goodyear
- Harley-Davidson
- Mercedes-Benz
- Rolls Royce
- Toyota
- Yamaha

Non-profit
- Red Cross

Notes

1   Kerry, Kathleen, "GM warms up the branding iron," *Business Week,* September 23, 1996.

2   Kotler, P., *Marketing Management: Analysis, Planning and Control* (8th edn), Prentice Hall, Engelwood Cliffs, NJ, 1993.

3   Hill, Sam, I; McGrath, Jack & Dayal, Sandeep, "How to brand sand," *Strategy & Business,* Second Quarter, 1998.

4   Totonis, Harry, & Acito, Chris, "Branding the bank: the next source of competitive advantage," *Insights* series, 1998.

5   "Don't get left on the shelf," *The Economist,* July 2, 1994.

6   Hill, Sam, I; McGrath, Jack & Dayal, Sandeep, "How to brand sand," *Strategy & Business,* Second Quarter, 1998.

7   *Financial World,* September–October 1997 (based on a formula resembling one devised by Interbrand).

The Ultimate Brands

American Express

A merican Express established itself internationally as the inventor of the traveller's check, but the strength of its brand comes largely from a single, simple insight: with the right advertising, a piece of plastic can be transformed into a status symbol. Today, the American Express Blue Box logo is one of the most widely recognized corporate symbols in the world.

Positioned as exclusive, American Express has come to represent an aspiration. While other credit card companies are keen to encourage people to carry their products, American Express has always traded on the idea that it is an achievement to possess its card. In terms of branding, the company was years ahead of the competition.

Introduced in the USA in 1958, the classic green American Express card was the perfect complement to the first golden era of consumer brands. Proud owners could do their consumer spending without having to carry wads of cash around. The famous charge card spoke volumes about those who carried it. It was inspired by convenience but smacked of other privileges. It was chic and sophisticated to pay with plastic.

The growth of the credit industry allowed Americans to have their washing machines, automobiles and television sets a little sooner than they would otherwise have afforded. Branded credit has been with us in various forms ever since. The American Express card, however, was a charge card. It had to be paid off each month.

What American Express soon realized was that an individual's credit rating was a prestigious commodity. The card said more about the user than a wallet stuffed with dollar bills ever could. The realization laid the foundation for the development of the American Express brand.

With its famous slogans: "American Express – that'll do nicely"; and "Don't leave home without it," the company sought to establish the proposition that: anyone who is anyone has an American Express card. "Membership has its privileges" in more ways than one. The card offers a sense of financial security and cachet; it is an announcement that you have arrived. Difficult situations are effortlessly resolved by producing the magic card. Advertisements featuring famous business chiefs including Anita Roddick, Richard Branson and Terence Conran, have been designed to strengthen this image.

Have brand will travel

The American Express Company began life as an express freight company The company traces it origins back to 1851. It was created by the union between a number of express carriers – Wells & Co., Livingston & Fargo, Butterfield, and Wasson & Co. – and first operated under the slogan "safety & dispatch" with a bulldog logo.

During the American Civil War, the company served the winning side and, in the 1860s, transported vital supplies to Union army depots. Later it took a hand in the spread of democracy, issuing ballot papers to troops in the field.

In 1882, as shipping large quantities of cash became increasingly hazardous, the company underwrote its first money order. The practice grew rapidly and American Express established relationships with a network of banks across Europe, building a business out of the transfer of funds from the growing numbers of immigrants settling in America and sending money home to their families in Europe.

Its reputation for financial services was growing, but the company remained predominantly a freight delivery operation. That changed in 1891, with the issue of the American Express Traveller's check – the first of its kind. This represented a major innovation: for the first time, the company was able to promise that a check written in dollars could be converted to a variety of other currencies. Best of all, it was automatically refundable if stolen or lost.

The arrival of the traveller's check freed the traveller to move across currency frontiers. The power of the traveller's check, however, resided in the power of the issuer's brand. This laid the foundations for the company's move into travel services. American Express began selling travel tickets for railroad and transatlantic ships.

When war broke out in 1914, 150,000 Americans found themselves trapped in Europe. Who could they turn to for help? American Express offices were besieged by panic-stricken US citizens desperate to get home. The company rose to the occasion. It posted money to points all across Europe. It is testament to the strength of its brand that in some countries, the locals preferred to trade in American Express traveller's checks rather than trust the local currency.

Its reputation was boosted still further in the 1930s during the Great Depression when the company continued to cash its traveller's checks despite the fact that many US banks were closed and their assets frozen. The American Express brand was more reliable than money.

Membership has its privileges

In 1986, when Amex took up residence at its new headquarters at the World Financial Center in New York, it seemed a fitting setting. Today, the company has three main businesses: travel; financial services; and communications.

By far the largest part of the empire is the travel related services business, which generates around half of the company's total profits. This part of the business operates the charge card for which the company is best known. Membership comes in three levels of privilege: the original green card; the gold card – which warrants an extra degree of personal service; and the Platinum card – which is only available to certain hand-picked individuals.

Amex's branding put it ahead of the financial services industry. It was only at the beginning of the 1990s that the rest of the financial services world discovered branding. Suddenly, television screens were filled with minor celebrities, colorful images and snappy lines. Customers were bombarded with cheerful messages about which bank to go with. They could choose from: the "listening bank," the "bank that likes to say yes" or the one which made sure their money was "never knowingly invested in companies that don't care about the environment."

The script was simple – banker meets advertising executive and it is love at first sight. In 1992 and 1993 UK spending on advertising in financial services increased by 33 percent. In 1994 it went up even faster by 36 percent. It was a similar story elsewhere. Financial services companies also discovered that they had customers and a huge amount of information about them – database marketing beckoned.

Meanwhile, despite some impressive deals, Amex was struggling. In 1993, the company acquired the travel agency business of Thomas Cook, making it the world's largest business travel agent. In the same year, it won the contract for the US federal government's travel and transportation payment system – which amounted to the world's largest corporate card account. Elsewhere the news was less upbeat.

An almost dysfunctional management team led by CEO James Robinson III damaged the Amex brand. Robinson's grand strategy to turn the company into a financial supermarket collapsed. In 1993, Robinson was replaced as CEO by Harvey Golub, but not before the company's Shearson Lehman brokerage subsidiary had eaten up around $4 billion in capital before being sold off. More trouble came from the American Express card, which lost market share to Visa and MasterCard.

Despite these setbacks, Interbrand, the London marketing group, insisted that American Express remained one of the true "super brands." In 1995, investment guru Warren Buffett, took a 10 percent stake in the company, claiming that Wall Street's low valuation of the company's stock failed to take account of the power of the brand, which he said was "synonymous with financial integrity and money substitutes around the world."

Golub's strategy was to build on the Amex name to "become the world's most respected service brand." Despite the introduction of its Optima card – a credit card to complement its traditional charge cards – the company missed out on the credit card bonanza in the late 1980s and early 1990s, and saw its market share decline. As new credit card issuers such as Advanta, Capital One and MBNA moved into the market, and players such as AT&T offering no fee plastic, so the market became more commoditized.

This was bad news for American Express which had always traded on prestige to justify premium fees. At the same time, retailers complained about the large bite the company took out of purchases. The dilemma for Golub was how to grab more market share without losing the American Express cachet. As David Aaker, marketing professor at U.C. Berkeley told *Fortune* magazine: "When you move downmarket you run the risk of losing what you had, and then you don't have anything."

More than two million American Express holders cut up their cards in the early 1990s. Just a few years later, however, things were looking up. While many of the newcomers were packing their bags and leaving the market, American Express was flying high. In 1997 it reversed a decade long slide in the US by winning back market share. The company added more cards for consumers to raise its share of the $469 billion general purpose card market.

Amex's master plan is to transform the credit card business by offering cards issued by banks. Despite delays caused by legal niceties in the US, the company has already signed up a network of leading banks in 19 other countries, including NatWest in the UK and Credit Lyonnais in France. The aim of the new game is to take the Amex brand to the masses. The question remains whether the ultimate in financial prestige brands can make the leap.

Card carrying

- 1851: The American Express Company began life as an express freight company created by the union between a number of express carriers.
- 1860s: American Express distributes ballot papers to civil war soldiers in the field.
- 1891: American Express invents the traveller's check.
- 1914: On the day World War One breaks out, the line at the famous American Express office at 11, Rue Scribe, in Paris is 100 metres long and six people deep as Americans try to get out of Europe.
- 1930s: American Express continues to cash its traveller's checks despite the fact that banks are closed and many have their financial assets frozen.
- 1958: American Express "green card" is introduced.
- 1986: Moves to its headquarters at the World Financial Center, New York.
- 1993: Acquires the travel agency business of Thomas Cook, making it the world's largest business travel agent.

W hen Apple launched the iMac, the stylish Internet ready computer which it hoped would re-energize the company's fading fortunes, "Chic. Not geek" was blazed across advertising posters. Beneath it were the Apple logo and the slogan "Think different." The campaign epitomized the enduring appeal of the Apple brand.

For a time, Apple was quite simply the hippest thing in computers and corporate America. Founded in a garage by two college dropouts – Steve Jobs and Steve Wozniak – the company changed the face of computing with the Apple 1 and Apple 2. Apple was all about making computers accessible to ordinary people. In a market where design went little further than beige boxes, the Apple machines stood out from the crowd. For a while they managed to scoop up 20 percent of the market.

Ownership of an Apple machine was a statement of identity: it was jeans and sneakers versus the suit and ties of corporate America. Apple had attitude. The two friends eventually fell out, with Wozniak leaving the company to become a teacher, but Jobs went on to launch the Apple Macintosh, with which he hoped to conquer the computer world. The crown went instead to Bill Gates whose Microsoft persuaded 80 percent of computer buyers to use its operating system MS-DOS rather than buy Apple.

Many industry commentators still believe that Apple could have been sitting where Microsoft is today. That battle is over, but whether Bill Gates won it or Steve Jobs blew it remains an open question. Observers agree that an important mistake Apple made was refusing to licence its operating system to other computer manufacturers. This left the door open for Microsoft's MS-DOS alternative. Some claim, too, that the company with attitude developed a little too much of the wrong sort of attitude, becoming arrogant and complacent.

After its early triumphs (the revolutionary nature of which cannot be under estimated), a series of false starts, missed opportunities and product flops saw Apple's market share dwindle, despite the enduring appeal of the Apple name and high brand loyalty. In recent years, Apple's very survival has been in question after a succession of comeback attempts went wrong. Jobs himself was kicked out of the company in 1985, only to return 13 years later to take up the post of "interim CEO." It remains to be seen whether the second coming of Jobs will resurrect the fortunes of his famous creation.

Upsetting the Apple cart

Like all the best computer companies, Apple began life in a garage. In 1977, Steve Jobs conceived the Apple 1, regarded by many as the first real personal computer. Jobs and his technically brilliant partner Steve Wozniak built the first machine and founded the Apple company. The Apple 2 followed, and then the Apple Macintosh.

Instead of writing commands in computerese, Macintosh owners used a mouse to click on easily recognizable icons – a trash can and file folders, for example. Suddenly, you didn't need a degree in computer science to operate a personal computer. Other companies followed where Apple led – most significantly Microsoft. But while Apple remained the darling of the creative world, Bill Gates and crew never achieved the same iconoclast status.

One newspaper described Jobs as a "corporate Huckleberry Finn" (begging the question: who was the corporate Tom Sawyer?) and said his early business exploits had already made him part of American folk history. The fairytale story came to a sticky end in 1987 when former Pepsi chairman John Sculley, who had been brought in to add some corporate know-how to the wilting Apple, removed Jobs.

Sculley himself was booted out in 1993 after a disastrous period that saw Apple's market share plummet from 20 percent to just eight percent. He was replaced by Michael Spindler, who lasted until 1996, by which time market share had fallen to just five percent. Apple was staring oblivion in the face as its long-term devotees began to switch to the Microsoft-powered PCs.

Spindler was shown the door, and Gil Amelio stepped into the hot seat. After 500 days in post, Apple's market share had fallen to four percent and Amelio invited Jobs to come in and help. With two being a crowd, Amelio soon made his exit and got down to the real business of writing a book about his experiences.

After a 13-year exile, Jobs was back. The iconoclast who founded the computer company with attitude was now its only hope of survival. The wheel had come full circle. The world has changed in the intervening period, but the Apple brand and the style of its famous founder remain well matched.

Baking fresh Apple pie

Since Jobs has been back at the helm, Apple has looked more like its old self. The iMac, a vision in translucent blue, sold 278,000 units in the first six weeks, an achievement that had *Fortune* magazine describing it as "one of the hottest computer launches ever." Wall Street, too, seems to have recovered its confidence in Apple – the company's share price doubled in less than a year.

Being Apple, there is unseemly squabbling about who is the architect of its (perhaps brief) renaissance. The spurned CEO, Gil Amelio, claims that Jobs stepped in at just the right time, and that he, Amelio, took on a moribund company and turned it around. The Amelio angle is that he bequeathed a re-energized Apple, with $1.5 billion in the bank and a number of stunning new product lines including the iMac.

The Jobs fans say the once and future king of Apple came in and saved the day. His actions since becoming self-styled "interim CEO" include dumping the NeXT operating system that he sold to Apple, dumping loss-making licensing contracts, and spotting the potential of the iMac.

Whatever the machinations behind it, the new machine is the embodiment of everything Jobs believes in: eye-catching design, and simple operation. The iMac is also the product of a different vision of the computer industry. It doesn't have a disk drive – because Jobs believes they have been superseded by external storage devices such as zip drives. Nor does the Apple CEO subscribe to the common view that the PC and TV are moving together. Whether Jobs or his nemesis Bill Gates proves correct on this could determine the future of both companies.

In the meantime, the iMac looks the best chance to restore Apple's fortunes. Apple owners have always been passionate, fierce even, in their belief that Jobs builds a better mouse trap. Brand loyalty has always been high. The best news of all for Apple is that some 40 percent of iMac sales are to new customers. This suggests that the iconoclast Apple brand can seduce a new generation of computer buyers.

Apple's bruising ride

- 1977: Steve Jobs and Steve Wozniak found Apple in a garage and go onto build the Apple 1, regarded by many as the first true personal computer.
- 1980: Apple goes public on the strength of the success of the Apple 1 and Apple 2.
- 1984: The Apple Macintosh computer is launched.
- 1985: Steve Jobs exits.
- 1987: Apple launches the Mac II.
- 1992: Apple loses copyright ruling in its lawsuit against Microsoft.
- 1993: Launches the Newton personal assistant. Newton flops. John Sculley leaves.
- 1995: Launches new laptops, but forced to recall them after two burst into flames. Profits drop by 48 percent.
- 1996: Market share drops to 5 percent. Gil Amelio in charge for 500 days. Steve Jobs returns.
- 1998: iMac is launched.

Barbie

O ften said to be the most successful toy in history, Barbie celebrated her 40th birthday in 1999. The world rejoiced. "Forty years of dreams" proclaimed Barbie's makers, Mattel. Forty or not, Barbie defies the ageing process in a defiantly old fashioned sort of way. No cellulite in sight, Barbie has long legs and a figure as shapely as shapely could be. Translated from doll size into reality, Barbie would stand seven feet tall with five feet long legs. Her stats would be 40–22–36. One might have thought that the sexist freak show Barbie-style would now be outdated. After all, children have PCs and Gameboys. Not so. A Barbie is bought every two seconds. Barbie, who first saw the light of day at the annual Toy Fair in New York in 1959, is now a $1.9 billion industry.

Barbie was the idea of Ruth Handler, wife of Elliott Handler, one of the founders of the toy company Mattel. Mrs. Handler saw her daughter playing with paper dolls and was inspired to make something a little more permanent and realistic. "If a little girl was going to do role-playing of what she would be like at 16 or 17, it was a little stupid to play with a doll that had a flat chest. So I gave her beautiful breasts," said Mrs. Handler. (The Handlers eventually sold most of their interests in Mattel in 1989.) The breasts haven't always worked in Barbie's favor. In Japan sales were initially sluggish. Market research found that girls and their parents thought that Barbie's breasts were too large. Mattel eventually changed the doll for the Japanese market. The licensee in Japan quickly sold two million of the smaller breasted Barbie.

Renaissance woman

Though Barbie is a universal and (usually) standardized product, part of its success has been the number of costume variations on offer. Over 100 new costumes are added each year. This is necessary because Barbie is a Renaissance woman. You can have it all. Just look at Barbie – "She's a successful businesswoman, a member of a rock band, and a Women's World Cup Soccer Player," Barbie's web site informs us. And she also has a man in her life, Ken. He is suitably coincidental. Introduced in 1961, Ken has lurked in the background, content presumably to see Barbie make such a success of her multi-faceted life. Barbie also has her friend, Midge, who first saw the light of day in 1963 before slipping into obscurity prior to a stunning 1988 comeback.

Barbie has moved with the times. Indeed, she has embraced virtually every fad and temporary fashion with something approaching abandon. Barbie was inspired by the Beatles, then became, of all things, a Mod. She has also, along the way, reflected the "prairie look," whatever that may be, and been into disco music. In the 1980s, she got into power dressing. She still found time to be an aerobics instructor. This sporting theme has continued. The late twentieth century Barbie is a basketball and soccer player.

Barbie's makers are proud of Barbie's multi-career approach. "Barbie has the unique ability to inspire self-esteem, glamour, and a sense of adventure in all who love her," Mattel gushes. "She has been a role model to women as an Astronaut in 1994, 1986 and in 1965 – nearly 20 years before Sally Ride! As a college graduate in 1963, surgeon in 1973, business executive in 1986, 'Summit Diplomat' and airline pilot in 1990, a presidential candidate in 1992, and a dentist in 1997, the Barbie doll has opened new dreams for girls that were not as accessible in the early 1960s. As a matter of fact, the world's most popular fashion doll has actually had 75 careers since her inception." Unfortunately, Mattel does not record the success of the Career Diplomat version.

Now Mattel, the Californian maker of the doll on perpetual heat, has entered the fashionable world of mass customization. Barbie now comes complete with 15,000 combinations. Change the outfit, the eyes, the color – but don't even think about the legs. All for $40 (double the usual price).[1] The management gurus were right. Mass customization is child's play.

Stretching Barbie

Barbie should have stretch marks, given the number of times the Barbie brand has been extended. Extensions include:

- 1961: The advent of Ken, the man in Barbie's packed life.
- 1963: Midge, Barbie's friend, invented to provide a shoulder to cry on. (Reborn in 1988.)
- 1964: Skipper, Barbie's little known younger sister.
- 1968: Barbie pushes back the cultural frontiers with her black friend, Christie.
- 1988: The Hispanic friend, Teresa, becomes Barbie's confidante.
- 1990: Kira, Barbie's Asian friend.
- 1992: Barbie's much younger sister, Stacie.
- 1995: Unfeasibly young sister, Kelly.
- 1997: Becky, confined to a wheelchair.

Note

1   *The Times*, November 11, 1998 and www.barbie.com

Benetton

I n 1965 Giuliana Benetton decided to knit a brightly colored sweater. If only she'd known where it would lead. Over 30 years on, Giuliana and her three brothers, Luciano, Gilberto and Carlo, have a global retail chain of 7000 stores in 120 countries selling brightly colored sweaters. Giuliana controls the work of over 200 designers at Benetton's Design Center. The company produces more than 200,000 garments a day.

Benetton is one of the most eye-catching brand arrivals of recent decades. Its success – latest worldwide annual sales were worth 2871 billion lire – has been built on three central platforms.

First, a simple but distinctive product. Benetton's trademark products – colorful clothing – are strikingly simple but instantly recognizable as the company's. It has extended its interests with caution. Its other brands now include Zerotondo, Sisley and 012. In 1997 it moved into sportswear and sporting equipment through such brands as Prince, Nordica and Rollerblade.

Second, highly distinctive advertising. The "United Colors of Benetton" brand provides a large variety of easy options for advertising images. Eschewing them, Benetton has cornered the market in surprising, or offensive, advertising. One features Luciano Benetton naked except for the line "I want my clothes back." Then there are the shocking images of people dying. Gratuitous? Perhaps it is, but it has largely succeeded in cementing Benetton's niche as a colorful outsider.

Photographer Oliviero Toscani has been responsible for some of the most striking images used by Benetton. "Everything we do is about impulse, about guts," says Toscani. "That's what built Benetton; Luciano didn't test the market for a taste in colored sweaters." The ads are an expression of the brand, of the company and of Luciano Benetton.

This is how the company explains the images it uses to sell more sweaters: "Benetton's communication strategy was born of the company's wish to produce images of global concern for its global customers ... Benetton believes that it is important for companies to take a stance in the real world instead of using their advertising budget to perpetuate the myth that they can make consumers happy through the mere purchase of their product." True enough, but Benetton's "stance" is often difficult to determine.

Third, huge investments in logistics and production to lower production costs and, more importantly, to be immediately receptive to changes in the marketplace. This has proved highly important in moving Benetton forward with the times.

For example, Benetton was outsourcing and contracting out work, long before it became fashionable. As long ago as 1982, Benetton contracted work out to 200 units of which the company owned a mere nine.

"Benetton achieves a major advantage over its competition because of its ability to 'micro-market' to individual retailers on a quick-response, just-in-time basis," says marketing guru, Philip Kotler. "Benetton's logistical advantage results in much lower inventories and warehousing costs, and its profits are 30 percent higher than the US apparel industry average. Benetton owes a large part of its success to its high investment in information power."[1]

The most crucial decision in this area was in 1992, when Benetton had a turnover in excess of £1 billion and appeared to have the world at its feet. At the time, Benetton was, according to the company anyway, the third best known brand in the world. But Luciano Benetton wanted to move the company forward. At the company's headquarter in Ponzano Veneto, a seventeenth century villa just outside Castrette di Villorba, north of Venice, Benetton came up with a highly ambitious plan. In response to high labor costs, Benetton invested a massive £80 million in an advanced clothing factory. It installed state of the art systems – software tells the machines what to make in response to information coming directly from the company's stores worldwide.

Its investment in technology has made Benetton's Castrette industrial complex among the world's most advanced. The factory produces almost 100 million garments every year. It includes an automatic distribution system which handles over 30,000 packages every day. This process is managed by a mere 19 people – a traditional system would require at least 400.

Benetton is now taking its brand to bigger and bigger stores. It has opened megastores in major European cities and its US flagship is the 1200 square meter store in New York's Scribner Building on 5th Avenue. Its support systems and studious awareness of how it is pushing and pulling its brand mean that, in Benetton's case, bigger may well become better.

Note

1   Kotler, Philip, *Marketing Management,* Prentice Hall, Englewood Cliffs, NJ, 1994.

*B*udweiser

udweiser's vital statistics are as impressive as the product is fizzy. It is the world's biggest beer brand accounting for a massive 22 percent of the industry's sales in the USA. Budweiser, together with other beers made by Anheuser-Busch, accounts for almost 10 percent of the total volume of beer consumed worldwide. Anheuser-Busch produces more than 50 percent more beer every year than its nearest competitor, Heineken.

Like many of the other top global brands, Budweiser has its origins in the US. Importantly, despite expansion worldwide, Anheuser-Busch has retained the brand's American roots. Budweiser is the beer workers have when they stop off at a bar on the way home from a hard day's work. The brand is associated with overalls, oily hands, hard work and traditional play. It is the beer for the ball game. Bud is the drink of the working guy in America. It is significant that Budweiser uses Clydesdales, strong work horses rather than thoroughbreds, in its commercials. (Indeed, such was the significance of this that it reputedly took two years to reach a decision.)

Quintessentially American it may be, but Budweiser's history is dogged by a decidedly un-American sub-text. It was in 1876 that Anheuser-Busch decided to use the name Budweiser – after a type of beer from a place called Budweis in an obscure outpost of the Austro-Hungarian Empire. Budweis has since evolved into Ceske Budejovice in the Czech Republic. While its name and its rulers have changed, this small town retains its brewing tradition. Indeed, the modern Czech company, Budejovicky Budvar is some 700 years old. It enjoys a healthy local market. The Czechs drink beer as enthusiastically as tap water – their average consumption of 160 liters a year is the highest per capita in the world. Budvar flourishes and, much to Anheuser-Busch's annoyance, has the legal right to use the Budweiser name in over 40 countries.

The legal wrangling between the American giant ("The King of Beers" according to its slogan) and the Czech minnow ("The Beer of Kings" according to its slogan) has been rumbling on for decades. The Czechs remain irritants, unwilling to roll over and take the dollars on offer. It is for this reason that in some countries, the Budweiser brand is marketed as Bud.

King of the world

While the Czech company has been a fly in the beer, it has not prevented Budweiser conquering the world. Budweiser's global ambitions are comparatively recent. It was not until 1981 that Anheuser-Busch formed an international division and began the process of selling Budweiser beer in the international marketplace. It has supported its global ambitions with very deep pockets.

Budweiser's branding has helped it become an American icon. Anheuser-Busch defines an icon in two ways – as a visual representation of an ideology or symbolic world and as a trademark that represents more than simply a brand name. Budweiser is routinely seen as the pre-eminent US beer. International associations with the US fall into two camps. On one hand there are the positive perceptions of America as vast, free and independent. On the other hand, America can be seen as the proponent and the origin of the junk fast-food and faddish culture.

To ensure that its brand was successfully positioned across international markets, Anheuser-Busch first developed a positioning statement. This defined what the company wanted the brand to represent and became the basis for all its international marketing activity. Its position was simply that Budweiser is a premium quality beer with a distinctively refreshing taste; Budweiser represents and lets beer drinkers in other countries be a part of the American image they like; and Budweiser is a popular beer worldwide.

Simple enough. This was supported in a number of ways. First by visuals and slogans. Budweiser has a very strong visual image – the symbolic world of the brand. This includes the label – widely recognized and very American with its red, white and blue colors; the Budweiser bow-tie logo; the long-neck bottle – akin to the Coke bottle in its distinctiveness; the slogans *King of Beers* and *The Genuine Article*.

The third element in the branding of Bud internationally was its brand personality, a series of images which provide a basis for local beer drinkers to relate to the brand. The Budweiser brand personality could be defined as all-American, masculine, active, social and genuine – consistent with a premium quality image. Luckily for Budweiser, being masculine, active, social, and genuine is not an American monopoly.

The fourth aspect of Bud's branding is the sheer scale of its marketing. It meets consumer expectations of a big brand. When Budweiser is launched in a country, it is a big deal. The company puts its money where its brand is through aggressive distribution and point-of-sale merchandising as well as association with large-scale events such as the soccer World Cup. (Typically, Bud spent $32 million to be "an official partner" of the 1998 World Cup.[1])

Having conquered the world outside the Czech Republic, Budweiser has more recently been tackling an equally difficult problem – the fact that its drinkers are becoming older and its image may increasingly be out of step with the needs and aspirations of younger beer drinkers. Among its responses was a TV ad campaign featuring frogs. Off-beat and wacky, it was targeted at a much younger audience. The Budweiser Frogs commercial was highly rated. It was a clever piece of advertising, but may well have worked against the brand's traditional strengths. While frogs have, somewhat strangely, great emotional appeal, they have absolutely nothing to do with the heartstrings of Budweiser's target market.

Guys in overalls tend not to be the greatest admirers of wacky frog-based humor. Coors and Mountain Dew drinkers, who like to think of themselves as irreverent and different, may well have appreciated the frog ad. As it was the frogs did little for Budweiser. Evolving the strengths of this remarkably long-lived brand to fit the younger generation remains a sizeable – and so far unmet – challenge.

Mine's a Bud, I think

Over the years, Budweiser has worked through a host of slogans. The one that has lasted longest is "King of Beers" – over 40 years and still running. Others have come and gone. Here they are, in chronological order from the very first bottle:

- King of Bottled Beers
- King of All Bottled Beers
- The Old Reliable
- Budweiser Means Moderation
- Old Time Flavor
- Make This Test – Drink Budweiser for Five Days
- America's Social Companion
- Budweiser – Everywhere/Live Life ... Every Golden Moment of It/Enjoy Budweiser ... Every Golden Drop of It
- Budweiser – A Beverage of Moderation
- A Perfect Host to a Host of Friends
- Food's Favorite Companion
- Budweiser is Something More than Beer...A Tradition
- It Lives With Good Taste Everywhere
- There's Nothing Like It – Absolutely Nothing
- King of Beers
- When You Know Your Beer ... It's Bound to be Bud
- Where There's Life ... There's Bud
- This Calls for Budweiser
- That Bud...That's Beer
- Beer Talk
- Budweiser is the King of Beers (But You Know That)
- Budweiser is the Best Reason in the World to Drink Beer
- When You Say Budweiser, You've Said It All
- Somebody Still Cares About Quality
- When Do You Say Budweiser?
- This Bud's For You

- Nothing Beats A Bud
- Proud to Be Your Bud.

Note

1   Hornik, Richard, "Can they be buddies?", *Time*, July 13, 1998.

Coca-Cola

I n May 1886 in Atlanta, Georgia a pharmacist called Dr John Styth Pemberton came up with a brain tonic. John Pemberton's brain tonic contained a leaf from a South American tree and West African seeds as well as caramel, phosphoric acid and a combination of seven "natural flavors" which remains a well-protected secret to this day. Pemberton's book-keeper, Frank Robinson, named it Coca-Cola. Robinson also wrote the name with a slanting flourish. (Meanwhile, in 1894 Caleb Bradham in North Carolina began to sell a drink he had developed to help relieve dyspepsia. It contained pepsin and evolved into Pepsi-Cola. But that's another story.)

Pemberton's drink was first sold at a soda fountain in Jacob's pharmacy in Atlanta by Willis Venable. It sold for five cents a glass. During its first year on sale, sales averaged six a day. This generated a grand first year's income of $50. Unfortunately, Pemberton had spent $70.

Today, more than 900 million Coca-Colas are sold every single day. Coca-Cola is the best known global brand. Currently it is available in virtually every country in the world – the only exceptions are Libya, Iran and Cuba where its absence is a matter of politics rather than taste.

The rise of the real thing

It is easy to assume that Coke became a global brand effortlessly in less sophisticated times. In fact, it became a global brand for a number of reasons.

First, it backed the brand from the very start. John Pemberton spent $73.96 on banners and advertising coupons during his first year. Coca-Cola realized the power of mass media long before many other much longer established companies. It has always advertised with gusto. According to the records, Coca-Cola's first ad appeared a mere three weeks after Pemberton invented the drink. Presumably the decision making chain was quite a short one. The ad ran in *The Atlanta Journal* and proclaimed:

"Coca-Cola. Delicious! Refreshing! Exhilarating! Invigorating! The New Pop Soda Fountain Drink, containing the properties of the wonderful Coca plant and the famous Cola nuts."

Later, Coke advertisements – proclaiming it to be "delicious and refreshing" – were featured in Georgia school reports.

Shortly before he died in 1888, Pemberton and his son sold the rights to Coca-Cola to Asa Candler (1851–1929). Candler – later Mayor of Atlanta – was also an advertising enthusiast (and, among other things, a doctor, pharmacist, property developer and entrepreneur). Among his initiatives was the distribution of thousands of vouchers giving free glasses of the drink. Soft drink; hard sell has been the central dichotomy of Coca-Cola's existence.

Coca-Cola's sales pitch was all-American. Early ads featured baseball star Ty Cobb and other ads provided idyllic views of American life. In 1931 Coke took this further by portraying Father Christmas as an enthusiastic drinker.

While Coke's advertising attracted customers, the packaging of the product also changed. Progress brought the curvaceous Coke bottle, one of the great images of the twentieth century. Of course, Coke hasn't actually used the bottle for a number of years but it is indelibly printed on our minds – indeed, if you buy a can of Coke there is still a picture of the bottle just to remind you of its beauty. The bottle was the result of a design competition held in 1915 and won by the Root Glass Company. (The competition, of course, was a smart marketing ploy.) The Coke president, Asa Candler, said: "We need a bottle which a person will recognize as Coca-Cola even when he feels it in the dark." The bottle differentiated the brand and added to the brand's identity. (Coca-Cola only became available in cans in 1955.)

Candler had actually sold bottling rights in 1899 to Benjamin Thomas and Joseph Whitehead for $1. Candler's children eventually sold the company to another Atlanta businessman, Ernest Woodruff for the then massive sum of $25 million. In 1923, Ernest's son, Robert Woodruff (1890–1985) became company president. During Woodruff's long tenure – surely one of the longest in corporate history – Coke continued to develop people's awareness of the product. Its Coke Bathing Girls calendars were a fixture in American drug stores during the 1930s. It looked further afield early on in its life. Indeed, it later looked to the skies – returning Apollo astronauts were welcomed with a sign reading "Welcome back to earth, home of Coca-Cola."

Humility has never been on the Coca-Cola agenda. One of its publicity handouts noted: "A billion hours ago, human life appeared on Earth. A billion minutes ago, Christianity emerged. A billion seconds ago, the Beatles performed on the Ed Sullivan Show. A billion Coca-Colas ago was yesterday morning." No post-modernist irony there.

Back on planet Earth, a foreign sales department was set up in 1926. Internationally, its reputation was cemented during World War II when it boldly and ambitiously promised that any US soldier would be able to buy a Coke for a nickel. Coke became the symbol of American taste and consumption. To fulfill its promise Coke built 60 mobile bottling plants and sent them along with the army. Each could be run by two men and produce 1370 bottles an hour. (The more cynical and worldly slant on this story is that Coke convinced the government that its drink was vital to the well-being and happiness of US troops to get around the potential threat of sugar rationing.)

The war cemented Coke's place at the heart of American society. *TIME* magazine celebrated Coke's "peaceful near-conquest of the world." (Coke's competitors complained of favoritism and hyperbole.) The post-war years saw Coke expand its corporate empire in the quest for what it engagingly called "share of throat." New drinks were added to its range. These included Fanta, Sprite and TAB. None hit the heights of the original brand.

In the 1970s doubt entered the Coca-Cola empire for the first time. Pepsi-Cola upped the pressure with the Pepsi Challenge. Coke had to open its eyes to the possibility that it had real competition.

After a remarkable reign, Woodruff gave way to Roberto Goizueta (1931–97) in 1981.

Goizueta was a Cuban who had escaped the country when Fidel Castro took over. He and his wife arrived in the US with 100 Coca-Cola shares and little else. Goizueta never sold the shares.

In most ways Goizueta's rule was a huge success. When he died in 1997, the company was valued at $145 billion compared with $4 billion when he had taken over the top job. Goizueta led Coke into the acquisition of Columbia Pictures in 1982. Though a nightmare to manage, this was one of the best deals in corporate history. In terms of sheer profit it is difficult to match. Just a few years later, Coca-Cola sold Columbia to Sony making a profit of nearly $1 billion. Goizueta also oversaw the successful launch of Diet Coke.

Unfortunately, Goizueta's time also included one of the great marketing gaffes of all time. In 1985 Coca-Cola announced to the world that it was replacing its traditional recipe cola with New Coke. In detailed research it had discovered that the new recipe was preferred by most consumers. It was, they said, smoother, sweeter and preferable to the old version. This conveniently overlooked the fact that the old version was selling in many millions every day of the week. To call this the marketing own-goal of the century would be to understate the effect only slightly. Coke was faced with a barrage of criticism. On the other hand, its arch-rival Pepsi could barely contain its glee – indeed, it quickly produced advertising which was extremely gleeful, rubbing in the fact that "the real thing" remained unchanged.

Realizing that its move had been disastrous, Coke back-tracked and, after 90 days, re-introduced the original coke. It has not been tinkered with since. Overall, however, Goizueta's leadership re-invigorated the Coke brand. Ill in hospital, Goizueta commented: "It's all right if people want to worry about me. But they shouldn't worry about the company, because it's in better shape than it's ever been."

Goizueta's reign was also significant on a wider plain. He did much to bring the concept of "value creation" to managerial attention. "At the Coca-Cola company, our publicly stated mission is to create value over time for the owners of our business. In fact, I would submit to you that in our political and economic system, the mission of any business is to create value for its owners," said Goizueta.[1]

Goizueta created value like few others have ever achieved. But what next? With a market capitalization of $142,164 million and an annual turnover of $18,868 million, Coca-Cola remains hugely robust. Interestingly, however, it is moving towards more adventurous brand stretching than it has previously succeeded in pulling off. In the 1980s it made an attempt to launch a clothing range with no less than Tommy Hilfiger (then unknown). It came to nothing. Now, Coca-Cola Wear is a reality. This is based on the belief that "consumers feel a special relationship with Coke that encompasses more than just the drinking experience." Perhaps, but even the strongest brand can soon become over-stretched if pulled in the wrong direction.

Drink up!

Coca-Cola's sloganizing has stood the test of time.

- 1886: Drink Coca-Cola
- 1904: Delicious and Refreshing
- 1905: Coca-Cola Revives and Sustains
- 1906: The Great National Temperance Drink
- 1917: Three Million a Day
- 1922: Thirst Knows No Season
- 1925: Six Million a Day
- 1927: Around the Corner from Everywhere
- 1929: The Pause that Refreshes
- 1932: Ice-cold Sunshine
- 1938: The Best Friend Thirst Ever Had
- 1939: Coca-Cola Goes Along
- 1942: Wherever You Are, Whatever You Do, Wherever You May Be, When You Think of Refreshment, Think of Ice-Cold Coca-Cola

- 1942: The Only Thing Like Coca-Cola Is Coca-Cola Itself. It's The Real Thing.
- 1948: Where There's Coke, There's Hospitality
- 1949: Coca-Cola... Along the Highway to Anywhere
- 1952: What You Want is a Coke
- 1956: Coca-Cola ... Making Good Things Taste Better
- 1957: Sign of Good Taste
- 1958: The Cold, Crisp Taste of Coke
- 1959: Be Really Refreshed
- 1963: Things Go Better With Coke
- 1970: It's The Real Thing
- 1971: I'd Like To Buy The World A Coke
- 1975: Look Up America
- 1976: Coke Adds Life
- 1979: Have A Coke And Smile
- 1982: Coke Is It!
- 1985: We've Got A Taste For You
- 1986: Catch The Wave
- 1989: Can't Beat The Feeling
- 1990: Can't Beat The Real Thing
- 1993: Always Coca-Cola

From the first drop

- 1886: John Pemberton invents a new drink.
- 1888: Following Pemberton's death, Asa Candler buys Coca-Cola.
- 1891: Candler buys complete control of the company for $2300.
- 1892: Candler and others form the Coca-Cola Company.
- 1893: Coca-Cola registered as a trademark.
- 1894: Bottled for the first time thanks to Joseph Biedenharn of Vicksburg.

- 1894: First outdoor ad.
- 1895: Sold in all US states.
- 1899: Opens first bottling plant.
- 1915: Contour glass bottle patented.
- 1919: Company sold to Ernest Woodruff's investment group for $25 million.
- 1940: Bottled in over 45 countries.
- 1943: Eisenhower asks for 10 bottling plants to supply US troops overseas.
- 1958: Fanta test marketed.
- 1960: Fanta introduced.
- 1960: Buys Minute Maid Corp.
- 1961: Sprite introduced.
- 1963: TAB launched.
- 1979: Mello Yello and Ramblin' root beer launched.
- 1982: Buys Columbia Pictures.
- 1985: New Coke introduced.
- 1992: Available in 195 countries.
- 1997: M. Douglas Ivester becomes only 10th company chairman following the death of Roberto Goizueta.

Note

1   Krass, Petre (ed), *The Book of Leadership Wisdom*, John Wiley, New York, 1998.

Disney

hicago-born, Walter E. Disney (1901–66) was brought up on a farm in Missouri before returning to Chicago to study art. In 1920, Disney moved to Kansas City where he worked for the animator Ub Iwerks. Along the way, Disney also went bankrupt with debts of $15,000 following the failure of his Laugh O Gram Company of Kansas City. In 1923 he left Kansas City for Los Angeles in search of a job in the movie business. He wasn't the first and he certainly wasn't the last. Initially, Disney was singularly unsuccessful. No job materialized. Disney thought he might have missed the boat entirely. "He was at least halfway convinced that he was too late, by perhaps six years, to break into animation, but [it] was the only area in which he had any prior experience," noted one of his later biographers.[1] Disney could have returned to Kansas. He didn't. Instead, he rented a camera, assembled an animation stand and set up a studio in his uncle's garage. In 1923, the 21 year-old Walt Disney was in business with his older brother Roy. In 1923 Disney, the corporation, was born.

Disney got off to a decidedly poor start. Its first film, *Alice*, barely kept the company going. The second, *Oswald the Rabbit*, came out in 1927. Walt's business acumen temporarily deserted him and he lost control of the product. Then his luck changed.

"I hope we never lose sight of one fact…that this was all started by a mouse," Walt Disney was fond of saying in his later years.[2] The origins of Disney's mousey inspiration are told in a myriad of variations. At one time it was reputed that in his early career he befriended a family of mice in his office. Alternatively, the *Daily Sketch* reported in 1938 that "On his way back to Hollywood in an upper berth he could not sleep. The continuous but slight creaking of the woodwork in his compartment sounded like a million mice in conference. The idea made him laugh and in that split second Mickey Mouse was born."

The mouse in question began life as Mortimer Mouse. Walt Disney's wife, Lilly, did not take to the name and suggested Mickey as a replacement. On Sunday 18 November 1928, Mickey Mouse featured in one of the only cinematic epics of seven minutes in length: *Steamboat Willie*. This was the first cartoon that synchronized sound and action.

Disney never looked back. *Flowers & Trees* (1932) brought the world Technicolor. By 1937, he was producing the feature length, *Snow White and the Seven Dwarfs*. More followed, including *Pinocchio* (1940), *Fantasia* (1940), *Dumbo* (1941) and *Bambi* (1942). After the war, Disney introduced his cartoon characters to real actors in classics including *Mary Poppins* (1964), *Davy Crockett* (1955) and *Treasure Island* (1950). The effect was much the same: huge success. This bred even greater ambitions. In 1955, Disney opened Disneyland in Anaheim, California. Disney World in Orlando, Florida opened in 1971.

Central to Disney's success was the culture created by Walt. It was strict – dress code, no swearing – and unforgiving. But it also created a completely separate world. When people began working for Disney they entered another world where, among other things, the language was different – typically, Disney employees are all cast members. People either loved it and stuck around or hated it and left.

The culture wasn't totally militaristic. In many ways, Disney was a far-sighted employer. In the 1920s, Walt had paid his creative team more than he himself was paid; in the 1930s bonus systems were introduced; training programs in the 1950s and, in the 1960s, Disney University was created. It has been accurately said that Walt Disney's greatest creation was Walt Disney the company.

Following Walt's death, Disney struggled in the 1970s. Then it took the brave decision (for Disney at least) to hire two outsiders – Michael Eisner and Frank Wells. They joined the company in 1984.

By that time, Disney was in poor shape. In 1983 its studios lost $30 million as excessively high costs took their toll. Attendances at Disney's theme parks were also on a downward slope.

Eisner, an ex-NBC clerk was a true believer and provided the energy and direction to resurrect the magic kingdom. Eisner's insight was that Disney is in the family entertainment business in all its manifestations. It wasn't just a movie company or a theme park operator. Eisner effectively widened Disney's perspective and ambit. He galvanized the brand into action. Disney launched Euro Disney and re-discovered its innovative powers. The Disney brand was stretched to encompass a mountain of merchandising, stores (10 in 1988 have mushroomed to over 630), books, videos, games, movies and theme parks.

Eisner proved a shrewd judge and a hard taskmaster. Fourteen of the first 15 movies produced under Eisner made money. In 1987, when *Three Men and A Baby* and *Good Morning Vietnam* became blockbusters, Disney had really turned the corner.

Eisner also proved adept at maximizing the profit potential of Disney's glorious back catalog. Between 1987 and 1990 he re-released classic after classic in special editions – *Snow White*, *Cinderella*, *Bambi*, *The Fox and The Hound*, *Peter Pan* and *The Jungle Book*. A new generation got to know Disney and, so long as the movies were in people's minds, merchandise could be sold.

Family entertainment became Disney's guiding light once more. The result was that Disney moved from being a $1.5 billion company in 1984 to a $22 billion company in 1997. "If you could have great entertainment and not as great profits, or great profits and not as great entertainment, I'll take the great entertainment every time," says Eisner in an unconvincing attempt to sound like Walt Disney himself. The reality is that great entertainment leads to great profits (and, of course, great salaries – Eisner's total income from Disney Corp in 1993 exceeded $200 million).

The Disney company is now the second largest entertainment company in the world. Its theme parks continue to attract vast numbers of people. Walt Disney World brings in 32 million visitors a year; Disneyland 14 million; Disneyland Paris 3 million; and Disneyland Tokyo 5.2 million. The 1995 acquisition of Capital Cities/ABC for $19 billion cemented its place among the entertainment elite.

Even so, complacency would be dangerous for its 108,000 cast members. Its 1997 operating profit was $1.03 billion (down by a worrying 31 percent) on revenues of $6.5 billion. With competition from Dreamworks – creator of the movie hits *Antz* and *Prince of Egypt* – Disney's heartland of children's entertainment is under fire as never before.

Disney jobs

Every year, Disney execs are supposed to spend a week working on the frontline. This in Disney argot is "cross utilization." When it comes to jobs, Disney has a language all of its own, which makes PC look positively indiscrete.

- *Cast members:* humble employees
- *Guests:* money-paying customers
- *Food & Beverage Hosts:* restaurant workers.
- *Transportation hosts:* drivers
- *Security hosts:* Disney cops
- *Custodial hosts:* Street cleaners.

Notes

1   Schickel, Richard, *The Disney Version,* Simon & Schuster, New York, 1968.
2   Holliss, Richard & Sibley, Brian, *The Disney Studio Story,* Octopus, San Francisco, CA, 1988.

Federal Express

O n April 17, 1993, 14 small aircraft took off from Memphis International Airport, carrying some 186 packages. On that night, an idea for an express delivery business that started life as a Yale term paper became a reality called Federal Express.

"Don't just send it, FedEx it," is a slogan that millions of customers have taken to heart since the company arrived on the delivery scene. Every morning in over 200 territories around the world, the purple and orange vans of Federal Express begin their daily race against deadlines. Back at base, their movements can be tracked almost minute-by-minute on computer screens as they thread their way through the traffic and disappear into offices. On their return, the couriers can get instant feedback on their performance compared against "expected efficiency."

Today, FedEx is the world's largest express transportation company, with 624 aircraft and service to over 211 countries. There are 46 call centers across the globe handling over 500,000 telephone calls daily. FedEx employs over 145,000 people, including 42,500 couriers who deliver more than 3.1 million packages every single working day.

In 1997, *Fortune* ranked Federal Express as the most admired company in its industry (package, freight delivery and mail). The *Fortune* global most admired ranking, which has become the business equivalent of the Oscars, put the FedEx brand alongside other global brands such as Coca-Cola, Microsoft and Toyota.

Growth with a friendly face

FedEx was started in 1971 when founder Fred Smith bought two

Falcon jets for $3.6 million. Smith's business was launched with the apparently brash promise of "guaranteed overnight delivery."

From a rich Memphis family, Smith is an ex-marine (with two Purple Hearts) who served two combat tours in Vietnam. "I wanted to do something productive after blowing so many things up," he once said.[1] The business philosophy he established relies on a simple chain that puts people first. Hiring the right people and treating them well creates excellent service at prices customers are happy to pay, which leads to profits. This deceptively simple approach underpins the brand offering: "reliability with a friendly face."

Flexibility and reliability were critical to its brand offering from the beginning. The big players, such as UPS, were perceived as bureaucratic and faceless; FedEx aimed to be neither. In what seems a first glance an entirely commoditized market, FedEx works hard to differentiate its service. That means service offerings that add value to long term customers.

Typical of the company's foresight was a huge distribution center it established near Memphis to serve its big customers. This depot allowed the company to keep supplies of urgently needed items, such as medical supplies and computer components, on hand. They were stockpiled by FedEx customers, such as IBM, so that one quick telephone call meant the vital item could be dispatched to wherever it was needed. Through insights such as this, argues management writer Tom Peters, "FedEx has redefined mail order."[2]

"We are the clipper ships of the computer age," Smith has observed. It was a statement borne out by the events of 1997. FedEx was the chief beneficiary of the acrimonious 1997 UPS strike, caused by a stand off between UPS management and the Teamsters union.

The major players in mail order personal computers, such as Gateway 2000, Micron and Dell, had the foresight and clout to do deals with FedEx before the UPS strike took effect. The smaller players in the PC mail order business were caught out, and had to pay full price to get their machines to customers. For FedEx it was a simple case of demand outstripping supply. The company was so swamped with work at one stage that it was forced to refuse new customers. Better that way than to let new customers down.

The secret to managing the FedEx brand is deceptively simple. Smith has created systems that rely on people rather than the other way round. If you put people in charge – first employees, and then customers – the systems will evolve around them. Most complex operations try to do it the other way. They create rigid systems and then try to squeeze human beings into the gaps.

The FedEx approach relies on the commitment of the people who work for the company and make the systems work. FedEx employees proclaim their "purple blood" (purple is the dominant color in the company's logo). Most FedEx managers are promoted from front-line jobs – couriers, for example. They have customer focus built into the way they think. Computerized tracking systems sound like Orwell's Big Brother at work, but they have a liberating effect when used to provide additional information to the individual instead of as a form of control.

"In a service company, like ours, the perceptions of quality is influenced every time an employee interacts with a customer," says Smith. "If an employee can't answer a question or resolve a problem, or at least know where to get a problem solved expeditiously, the moment as well as the customer is easily lost."[3]

Smith himself has also managed to retain the edge that made the company successful in the first place. As Linda Grant noted in an article in *Fortune*: "Smith, unlike most entrepreneurs, has proven a durable manager. His hands-on, detail-oriented leadership has shaped every facet of corporate strategy."[4]

The downside of the FedEx model is that it is a very expensive business to run. Every year it spends between $2 billion and $2.5 billion. The company has installed computer terminals at 100,000 customers' offices. Using its customer information has enabled it to target its most lucrative accounts. It also maintains electronic communications with more than 750,000 customers.

By 2007, the world express transportation market could be worth some $150 billion against the current $12 billion. With its brand riding high, FedEx is in an ideal position to take advantage. The great unknown is what the impact of the Internet and electronic message delivery will have on a business that has traditionally been strong in document delivery.

The FedEx story

- 1973: Becomes the first company to offer overnight delivery in the US.
- 1974: Broadcast advertising of the Federal Express product launched in six local markets. After a single campaign, created for under $150,000, business increased from 3,000 packages a night to more than 10,000. Volume increased steadily over the next decade.
- 1986: First express company to introduce a money-back guarantee.
- 1988: Package volume reached 1 million a day.
- 1994: Achieves ISO 9001 quality certification for its entire worldwide operation, the *first* major carrier to be recognized in this way.
- 1996: Launches FedEx International First, an 8 am door-to-door delivery service to nearly 5000 zip codes across the US.
- 1996: Expands its European service, further improving the range of solutions offered to customers and its international operations.
- 1997: UPS strike gives FedEx's business a major boost.
- 1999: FedEx is the world's largest express transportation company.

Notes

1   His father founded the Dixie Greyhound Bus Company and was a multi-millionaire.
2   Peters, Tom, *Thriving on Chaos*, Macmillan, London, 1987.
3   Krass, Peter (ed), *The Book of Leadership Wisdom*, John Wiley, New York, 1998.

4   Grant, Linda, "Why FedEx is flying high", *Fortune*, 1997.

T
he GAP was one of the great retailing success stories of the 1980s. The brand appeals to consumers who want to be trendy without being fashion victims. To some extent, the GAP secret is the clever presentation of unexceptional but high quality casual clothes in an aesthetic package that is pleasing to the customer at a number of levels. These include, easy outfit co-ordination, a wide choice of color, and non-threatening store design.

A key part of the brand appeal is a sense of timeliness. The message is: the GAP helps you create a casual, comfortable look that moves with the times. The Christmas 1996 GAP slogan – "Every color – only GAP" – was the antithesis of Henry Ford's "Any color you like as long as its black."

Bridging the GAP

Founded in 1969, more than just about any other brand GAP is all about being contemporary without trying too hard. For a number of years it was content to sell Levi's jeans and identify itself with the lower case gap logo. In the 1970s and early 1980s, the enclosed mall shopping concept was really taking off and creating a recognizable retail outlet was a sensible strategy. But as the look of clothes retailing changed in the early 1980s, GAP began to look dated. Other retail stores had copied the GAP formula, using similar store design and selling look-alike products. Multicolored T-shirts and sweat shirts were piled high in many clothes stores which replicated the GAP feel and atmosphere. The original had to do something to preserve its position.

The company's CEO Millard "Mickey" Drexler realized it was time for The GAP to stop thinking of itself as a retailer and start thinking like a brand. The result is the creation of one of the star brands of recent years.

The company's turnaround under Drexler was impressive. In 1983, the company changed its logo to long, clean-limbed upper-case letters to become The GAP. So different was the new corporate identity that commentators have observed that the old logo seems to belong to a different company altogether.

By 1991, it had re-invented itself, dropping the Levi line altogether and creating its own branded clothing lines. But The GAP stores are only one part of the story. In the US, The GAP Inc. also revitalized Banana Republic – acquired in 1983, tired by the 1990s, since rejuvenated. GAP Inc. also introduced Old Navy Clothing stores in 1994, with a warehouse feel to the outlets.

In effect, the company fashioned three distinctive identities targeted at different market segments. At the top end, there is Banana Republic; at the lower end is Old Navy; and occupying the upper-middle ground is the GAP brand. Key to the brand offering in all three cases is freshness. The company is constantly introducing new colors and rotating its offerings to ensure that, whatever the season or the latest fashion, you can walk into its stores and find something that is entirely contemporary. The styles change far less frequently, and the average shopper knows that GAP purchases are solid purchases with a good wardrobe shelf life.

The company has successfully integrated marketing and advertising supported branding into its merchandising operation. The clean, uncluttered look that is the hallmark of the GAP brand image works just as well across age groups. With more than 1000 stores in the US Canada, France, Germany Japan and the UK, plus over 550 GAPKids and BabyGAPs, creatively, all the GAP branding has the same feel, and the same simple clothes designs.

Drexler's insight proved prescient. Since, 1994, when some commentators were writing the company off as a "mature business," sales have rocketed. "They made their name into a brand," notes one leading retailing analyst. "They are one of the few retailers who have that luxury."[1]

Once bitten by the branding bug, Drexler is said to have immersed himself in information about the world's leading brands, especially Coca-Cola. It is no coincidence that Sergio Zyman, a senior marketing executive from Coca-Cola, was invited to join the GAP board of directors. "The GAP accelerated to the point where the brand was on fire," the partisan Zyman has observed. "There is no competitor who has a kind of brand essence that can pose a threat."

The company is taking no chances. It is pouring advertising money into its brand strategy like gasoline to keep the flames high. In 1996, the company spent around $100 million; in 1997, it spent $150 million.

In 1995, recognizing the strength of its brand appeal, The GAP added a line of personal care products packaged with an upbeat stainless steel look that complemented the brand aesthetics and the no-nonsense feel of its stores.

The new product line smacked of quality, but affordable quality. It was designer design, without designer prices.

The management style of the company is also important. The corporate culture encourages a degree of risk taking, and mistakes are considered a learning opportunity. The company prides itself on its ability to make fast decisions without lots of management layers. "We decide, 'is it the right thing for the business?'" one executive at the company observed. "When The GAP decides to do something, we do it. That's a rare thing in a company."

The company also has a flair for PR. In September 1997, it organized the "GAP at Work" event. Executives from the company rang the opening bell of the New York Stock Exchange. The exchange has a shirt and tie dress code, but it allowed floor workers to wear the khaki chinos and blue shirts The GAP handed out.

In recent years, too, the company has shown a willingness to move with the times, embracing Internet shopping.

While there is a retro feel to the advertising that harks back to traditional American values, GAP appears to have learned from its crisis in the early 1980s of the dangers of becoming outdated. What customers get at a GAP outlet, as well as some pretty good clothes in a wide variety of colours, is the brand's unspoken promise not to be left behind – a second time. It is a triumph of conservatism over the fashion industry. The GAP brand promise is one of safe, comfortable clothes that will never embarrass the wearer. More than this, the company has successfully exported classic American style to parts of the world that had previously managed to resist it. It is not unusual, for example, to find teenagers in Rome, Paris or London dressed in GAP baseball caps and US style sweats.

Above all it is easy shopping. Stores offer easy access and garments are color co-ordinated for customers. The company's first major TV advertising campaign in 12 years was kicked off by rap artist LL Cool J. The rap? "How easy is this?"

Notes

1   Cuneo, Alice, "Marketer of the Year: The GAP," *Fortune*, December 1997.

General Electric

O f the great smokestack brands, General Electric (GE) is one of the few survivors. It has survived – and prospered as never before – because it learned how to leverage its brand. The GE of the new millennium is a creator and maximizer of brands. Its brands feed on and feed from each other.

The modern GE began life in December 1980, when Jack Welch was announced as the new CEO and chairman of GE. It was a record breaking appointment. At 45, Welch was the youngest chief the company had ever appointed. Indeed, he was only the eighth CEO the company had appointed in 92 years.

He took over a company which was a model for American corporate might and for modern management techniques. GE had moved with the times – though usually more slowly. When Welch became top man GE's net income was $1.7 billion. By most measures, the company was growing at a healthy rate – by nine percent in the previous year. Everything seemed rosy. More plain sailing was anticipated as the new chief got used to the job.

However, plain sailing was not on Jack Welch's route map. During the 1980s, Welch put his dynamic mark on GE and on corporate America. GE's businesses were overhauled. GE's workforce bore the brunt of Welch's quest for competitiveness. GE virtually invented downsizing. Nearly 200,000 GE employees left the company. Over $6 billion was saved.

Stage one of life under Jack Welch was a brutal introduction to the new realities of business. Perhaps Welch was too brutal. But, there is no denying that by the end of the 1980s GE was a leaner and fitter organization. Any complacency which may have existed had been eradicated. Having proved that he could tear the company apart, Welch had to move onto Stage Two: rebuilding a company fit for the twenty-first century. The hardware had been taken care of. Now came the software.

Central to this was the concept of Work-out which was launched in 1989. Welch has called Work-out, "a relentless, endless company-wide search for a better way to do everything we do."[1] Work-out was a communication tool which offered GE employees a dramatic opportunity to change their working lives.

Welch the destroyer became Welch the empowerer. Work-out was part of a systematic opening up of GE. Walls between departments and functions came tumbling down. Middle management layers had been stripped away in the 1980s. With Work-out, Welch was enabling and encouraging GE people to talk to each other, work together and share information and experience. At first surprised, they soon revelled in the opportunity.

The next stage in Welch's revolution was the introduction of a wide-ranging quality program. Entitled Six Sigma, it was launched at the end of 1995. Six Sigma basically spread the responsibility for quality. Instead of being a production issue it was re-cast as an issue for every single person in the company.

Back in 1981 as Jack Welch began life as CEO, GE had total assets of $20 billion and revenues of $27.24 billion. Its earnings were $1.65 billion. With 440,000 employees worldwide, GE had a market value of $12 billion.

By 1997, GE's total assets had mushroomed to $272.4 billion and total revenues to $79.18 billion. Around 260,000 employees – down a staggering 180,000 – produced earnings of $7.3 billion and gave the company a market value of $200 billion.

GE now operates in over 100 countries with 250 manufacturing plants in 26 countries. Its workforce totals 276,000 with 165,000 in the US. The company's 1997 revenues were $90.84 billion with net earnings of $8.203 billion. The company's market value (according to the 1997 annual report) was the highest in the world: $300 billion. As a total entity, GE was ranked fifth in the most recent *Fortune 500*. Nine of GE's businesses would be in *Fortune*'s top 50 if ranked independently. GE remains a corporate giant. And now, it appears to be big in all the right places.

Leveraging the GE brand

Jack Welch has said that "Our job is to sell more than just the box."[2] He has moved the company from industrialized service to customer intimacy. When he took over, GE's attitude to customer service was typical of a traditional manufacturer. "At one time, GE executives spent more time on company politics than they did on actual business. People said that GE operated with its face to the CEO and its ass to the customer," Welch quipped.[3]

Welch has turned things round. He has done so in a number of ways. First, GE has moved from being a manufacturer to a manufacturing and service business. In 1998 more than two-thirds of GE's revenues came from financial, information and product services. Central to this has been the development of its financial services operation.

As a new service, GE Capital has made the most of GE's strengths in other channels. By using the company's triple-A credit rating it has gained financial power its competitors can only dream of. Its base remains GE customers – retailers – and end consumers. From providing financing for GE equipment customers, GE Capital has become the largest issuer of private label credit cards for retailers and others. "We're trying to develop a culture that says the world is the marketplace – don't make distinctions by country. The distinction remains the type of customer, not the country," says GE Capital chairman, Gary Wendt. "The private label credit card business is really a marketing arm for retailers – we spend as much time dissecting customers' buying habits as their creditworthiness."

In the not too distant future, it is possible that GE Capital, which finances everything from washing machines to jet engines, will make more money than all the rest of the company's businesses combined. "GE Capital could get to be 50 percent-plus of the company," Welch has said.[4]

In 1996, GE Capital made after-tax profits of $2.8 billion on revenues of $33 billion. Of US financial services businesses only Citicorp, the American International Group and Bank America earned more.

The second element to this is that GE has worked hard at sustaining a variety of customer channels. It has developed better means of servicing and meeting the needs of smaller retail outlets to make their businesses sustainable in the face of intensifying competition from big retailers such as Circuit City.

In order to make smaller retailers more viable GE developed a distribution system involving five different mixing warehouses and 76 locations where products can be delivered to the retailer or end user. Its logistics network means that there is a one- to two-day delivery service. This allows retailers to reduce inventory so they only need display models. For the retailers this is a major leap forward as inventory usually used to tie up most of their assets. In addition, retailers are given the opportunity to take advantage of business loans, store remodeling kits as well as software to help them manage their stores more efficiently.

GE has effectively positioned itself as the retailer's partner rather than simply a supplier and has made the small retail sales channel viable and sustainable. By providing quicker service it made the channel more economically attractive and split the gains with the retailers.

Finally, GE has explored changing customer expectations in great depth. GE's customer service help desk, the GE Answer Center, has been used to help gather valuable market research on evolving product and service preferences.

The result of all this is that internal and external perceptions of GE has changed. Once upon a time, GE sold boxes. You went to your friendly retailer and bought a washing machine. That was that. Now, the washing machine is only a lure to get you into the GE empire of service. One brand leads to another and all come with the GE guarantee of quality. You buy the washing machine with credit from GE's very own credit company in a store kitted out at GE's expense. Your numbers and details are fed in. You walk out with the hardware while GE's software cranks into action. The box is increasingly incidental. Long live the brand.

The GE business

- *Aircraft engines*. In 1996–97, GE won 70 percent of the world's large commercial jet engine orders. It is the world's largest producer of large and small jet engines for aircraft.
- *Appliances*. GE Appliances sells over 10 million appliances in 150 world markets, including refrigerators, freezers, ranges, cooktops, wall ovens, dish washers and washing machines. Its brands include the Monogram, GE Profile, Hotpoint, RCA and private label brands.
- *Capital services*. GE Capital is the star in GE's firmament. From being a side line it has become a high performing diversified financial company.
- *Industrial systems*. Circuit breakers, switches, transformers, switchgear, meters, etc.
- *Information services*. Business-to-business electronic commerce solutions. GE manages the world's largest electronic trading community with more than 40,000 trading partners.
- *Lighting*. From halogen lamps to outdoor lighting, GE supplies lighting for consumer, commercial and industrial markets.
- *Medical systems*. Medical diagnostic imaging technology – including X-ray equipment.
- *Broadcasting*. GE owns the US television network NBC which has, among other assets, the US rights to the Olympics until 2008. Various other operations including CNBC and MSNBC.
- *Plastics*. Engineered plastics for a variety of industries including building and computing.
- *Power systems*. The design, manufacture and service of gas, steam and hydroelectric turbines and generators. And, controversially, nuclear fuels and services.

> • *Transportation systems.* Locomotives and similar products. GE makes more than half of the diesel freight locomotives in North America.

Notes

1   General Electric Annual General Meeting, 1990.
2   Smart, Tim, "Jack Welch's encore," *Business Week*, October 28, 1996.
3   Tichy, Noel, & Sherman, Stratford, *Control Your Destiny or Some-one Else Will*, Currency Doubleday, New York, 1993.
4   Waters, Richard, "Too big for its booties," *Financial Times*, October 9, 1997.

T he Gillette brand started life in 1901 on the Boston waterfront as the Gillette Safety Razor Company with the endearingly named King Camp Gillette (1855–1932) trying to persuade investors to put their money into a company with an untested product. It was not until 1903 that the company began production of its razor sets and blades. The idea had actually come to the highly entrepreneurial Gillette in 1895 – taking your time to get it right has been something of a characteristic of the company ever since.

During its first year, Gillette sold 51 razor sets and 168 blades. By 1905 it was selling 250,000 razor sets and nearly 100,000 blade packages. And, by 1915, sales had increased hugely once more so that the company was selling 7 million blades a year. In 1917 the US government placed an order for 3.5 million razors and 36 million blades. The entire army needed a shave. In 1923, Gillette produced a gold plated razor – a snip at a dollar. (By this time King Gillette had disappeared into the sunset – Los Angeles – to convert his experience into social theories.)

By the 1950s, Gillette could sponsor the World Series, announcing that it was "The only way to get a decent shave." Such confidence carried the business forward until the 1970s when it was hit by cheap competition and the 1980s when four attempts were made to buy the company.

Well groomed

Gillette could have been pushed relentlessly downmarket. For a while, it was, as cheap throwaway razors made their presence felt in its markets. Then it re-discovered its competitive advantage: quality. "The critics didn't understand the real problem. It was that Gillette had lost sight of what its brand was," observed Bradley Gale of the Strategic Planning Institute. "Marketers can create brand power and superior returns almost anywhere – if they focus on becoming perceived quality leaders."[1]

Since then the brand has carved out a lucrative niche for itself in what is labelled male and female grooming as well as in a number of areas, including alkaline batteries. Gillette's empire now includes Braun electrical appliances; toiletries and cosmetics; stationery products (it owns Parker and Papermate pens); Oral-B toothbrushes and the battery-maker, Duracell with which Gillette merged in 1996. Little wonder that it is estimated that over 1.2 billion people use a Gillette product every day. This explains why the company had 1997 sales of $10.1 billion and has 44,000 employees working in 63 facilities in 26 countries.

Gillette's fans include Warren Buffett who has commented: "I go to bed happy at night, knowing that hair is growing on billions of male faces."[2] For investors like Buffett, Gillette has a number of attractions. Most notably, Gillette appears to have struck a balance between innovation and the marketplace. "Good products come out of market research," says CEO Alfred Zeien. "Great products come from R&D. And blockbusters are born when something great comes out of the lab at the same time people want it."[3] Zeien – like Warren Buffett and King Gillette – takes the long view. He points to similarities between Gillette developing new products and the long-term R&D necessary to develop new drugs.

Gillette has proved adept at introducing new products which come to dominate the marketplace. Its most notable triumph of recent years has been the Sensor range of razors. Development of the Sensor actually began in 1979, but it wasn't introduced until 1990. Gillette spent $275 million on designing and developing the range. Sensor has been one of the great business successes of recent years – by 1995 it accounted for $2.6 billion in sales. With 68 percent of the US wet shaving market and 73 percent of the European market, competitors haven't made any inroads into Sensor's domination. Most have shrugged their shoulders and looked elsewhere for opportunities.

Gillette is truly global in its reach and operations. Over 70 percent of its sales and profits come from outside the USA. No less an authority than Rosabeth Moss Kanter has said that "Gillette does internationally what every company should be doing." Gillette can only hope that it continues to be so little emulated.

Close shaves

- 1901: Company founded in Boston by King C. Gillette.
- 1903: Manufactures first safety razor.
- 1905: Sales office in London opened. Manufacturing plant in Paris.
- 1918: Three and a half million safety razors, and 36 million blades supplied to the Armed Forces when the US Government decided to issue shaving equipment to servicemen.
- 1932: Gillette introduces its first blue blade.
- 1953: Introduces foaming shaving cream.
- 1960: Launches Right Guard deodorant aerosol.
- 1963: Patents coated stainless steel blade.
- 1967: Buys BRAUN AG.
- 1971: Introduces Trac II – the world's first twin-bladed shaving system.
- 1973: Annual sales exceed $1 billion for the first time.
- 1984: Buys Oral-B (the US toothbrush manufacturer).
- 1986: Major restructuring program.
- 1987: Buys Waterman, the French pen manufacturer.
- 1990: Pan-Atlantic product launch of the Sensor shaving system.
- 1993: Buys Parker Pens.
- 1994: *Financial World* magazine ranks Gillette as the ninth most valuable brand in the world.
- 1996: Merges with Duracell.
- 1998: Launches "Mach 3" triple bladed shaving system.

Notes

1   Peters, Tom, *Liberation Management*, Knopf, New York, 1992.
2   Grant, Linda, "Gillette knows shaving – and how to turn out,"
    Fortune, October 14, 1996.
3   Grant, Linda, "Gillette knows shaving – and how to turn out,"
    Fortune, October 14, 1996.

Goodyear

Charles Goodyear (1800–1860) was not one of earth's luckier inhabitants. But he was philosophical about his lack of good fortune: "Life should not be estimated exclusively by the standard of dollars and cents. I am not disposed to complain that I have planted and others have gathered the fruits. A man has cause for regret only when he sows and no one reaps."[1]

Goodyear developed the process of vulcanization. This turned rubber from an adhesive and largely impractical material into one that could be used for a huge variety of purposes. Goodyear himself used rubber for more purposes than are usually contemplated – among his many experiments were rubber hats, vests and ties; rubber banknotes; rubber books, etc. Goodyear believed in rubber, but was usually a little slow about registering his patents and a bit careless about business matters.

Of course, he hardly made a cent from all this brilliant inventiveness. At one point he and his family were living in the remnants of another failed rubber factory on Staten Island, kept alive by the fish Goodyear caught. Goodyear spent a great deal of time and money trying to fend off unscrupulous pirates who stole his ideas. At one point he seemed to have won. In 1852 the US Supreme Court ruled in his favor and outlawed any further infringements of Goodyear's patents. Goodyear cheerfully handed over $15,000 to his lawyer, none other than Daniel Webster. Unfortunately, the infringements continued and on his death, Goodyear had built up debts of $200,000.

It is no surprise therefore that the Goodyear Tire & Rubber Company, the world's largest rubber business, has no connection with Charles Goodyear at all, apart from borrowing his name. Goodyear was founded in 1898 by Frank A. Seiberling. From its first factory on the banks of the Little Cuyahoga River in East Akron, Ohio, it made horseshoe pads, bicycle and carriage tires, seating rings for canning, fire hose and even rubber poker chips. Goodyear got off to an immediately profitable start. Its first month's sales amounted to $8246 (remember that Coca-Cola only made $50 in its first year.)

In its early years, Goodyear got into car racing – it offered its tires to the boy-racer Henry Ford in 1901 and two years later PW Litchfield patented the first tubeless automobile tire. By 1926 Goodyear had sales of $230,000 and was the biggest tire and rubber company in the world. It had also acquired the patents to Zeppelins and built America's first rigid airships.

Goodyear's evolution into a global brand was, by most standards, relatively painless. It was not until the late 1980s that it really hit problems. First, during the 1980s it had to fend off unwelcome advances from potential purchasers. Its eye was off the ball. Replacement tire shipments fell from 18.9 million units in 1986 to 16.2 million in 1989. Goodyear's share of tires on new car shipments fell from 12.8 percent to 10.5 percent from 1986 to 1989. Profits from replacement tires were also heading downwards at the same time. In 1990 the company made a net loss of $38 million from revenues of $11 billion.

Goodyear's travails were symptomatic of the decline of American power in the tire industry. This was most potently demonstrated when the Japanese interloper, Bridgestone, bought the US tire company, Firestone.

The 1990s provided a continuing series of challenges for the Goodyear brand. Most notable among these was overcapacity in the tire business—estimated at 15 percent or more worldwide. One cost cutting exercise has followed another. In 1998 Goodyear's sales fell; 2800 lay-offs were announced. Goodyear now has over 95,000 employees; market capitalization of $8 billion; turnover of $13.1 billion; and (1997) profits of $558.7 million.

The most significant response to the problems in the industry that afflict Goodyear came at the beginning of 1999 when the company announced an alliance with its Japanese competitor, Sumitomo Rubber. With total 1997 sales of $4.7 billion, Sumitomo has rights to the Dunlop brand in major world markets. The alliance was aimed at achieving savings of $300 to $360 million. In addition, it combined Sumitomo's strength in Japan with Goodyear's strength in

North America and Europe. The new combination boasts 22.6 percent of the $69.5 billion world tire market, making it the leading player – Bridgestone manages 18.6 percent narrowly ahead of Michelin on 18.3 percent.[2] Whether the alliance will solve Goodyear's problems is debatable. But, as Charles Goodyear demonstrated, hope can spring eternal.

Goodyears and bad

- 1898: Company founded by Frank A Seiberling with factory in East Akron, Ohio.
- 1901: Enters car racing with Henry Ford.
- 1903: PW Litchfield patented the first tubeless automobile tire.
- 1924: Acquires patents to Zeppelins.
- 1927: Opens first European manufacturing plant.
- 1937: First American-made synthetic rubber tire built & tested.
- 1951: 500 millionth tire made; reaches $1 billion in sales.
- 1963: One billionth tire.
- 1970: Supplies first tires on the moon.
- 1976: Chemical divisions ships first shatterproof polyester resin soft-drink bottle (PET).
- 1983: Three billionth tire.
- 1986: Fights off hostile takeover bid.
- 1989: $64 million project to increase synthetic runner capacity.
- 1993: Becomes first tire store in Beijing and first Western tire company in China.
- 1994: First tire company with an electronic store; $20 million joint venture with the Qingdao Gold Lion Hose Co.
- 1997: $600 million investment plan to grow business including two new plants.
- 1999: Goodyear announces alliance with Japan's Sumitomo Rubber.

Notes

1   "Charles Goodyear and the strange story of rubber," *Reader's Digest*, January 1958.
2   "Tread carefully," *The Economist*, February 6, 1999.

"**P**ure genius," one of its most successful slogans, is an apt description of the Guinness brand. Through a combination of a distinctive quality product, imaginative advertising and the Irish gift for story telling, it has managed to persuade consumers that Guinness is the name of a black and white drink, rather than simply the brand name of a stout.

In Britain, Guinness has the highest spontaneous brand awareness of any beer brand. One million pints of draught Guinness are sold there every day. Such is the appeal of the black drink with its distinctive white head that people don't ask for stout, they ask for a pint of Guinness. The famous O'Neill harp logo, with the signature of the company founder Arthur Guinness was introduced in 1862, and is instantly recognizable to drinkers the world over.

Ever since its first campaign in 1928, Guinness has had a special place in British advertising. Over the years the brand has earned a reputation for some of the most creative campaigns, using famous artists and writers. At times, Guinness ads have transcended the divide between commercial images and popular art – something that complements its brand positioning.

Guinness is not traditional in the traditional sense; it is forward-looking and idiosyncratically cool. The appeal to younger drinkers is clear from the changing profile of Guinness drinkers. In 1987, the average age of a Guinness drinker was around 47; by 1997, it was under 35.

Irish roots

Guinness benefits greatly from its Irish heritage. The company was founded in 1759 by Arthur Guinness. He set up his operation in an abandoned brewery in Dublin. So sure was he that the company would succeed, the story goes, that he signed a 9000-year lease for the premises at £45 per year. Originally, the company made Dublin ale, but soon diversified into producing a relatively new beer called porter – a stout that took its name from the porters at Covent Garden who had a particular fondness for it. Roasted barley used in the brewing process gave the extra strong porter (known as a stout porter) made by Guinness its distinctive dark color. Within a few years, it had become known as Guinness stout.

Under the management of Arthur's three sons, the Guinness company began exporting its stout to other foreign markets. It was Arthur Guinness II who insisted that the company focus on using high-quality ingredients to create a beer that was both stronger and longer-lasting than other stouts. The famous brew became so popular with stout drinkers that by the early 1880s the St James Gate brewery was the largest in Ireland.

It got bigger. By the end of the nineteenth century, the Guinness brewery was the largest in the world. The company Arthur Guinness and Sons was floated on the London Stock Market and its brand exported to be enjoyed by consumers as far afield as North America, Australia and parts of Africa. As the new century opened, in step with the new mood of scientific endeavour, Guinness took brewing high-tech. The company established analytical and research laboratories in Dublin and employed science graduates straight from university. Interestingly, despite the appliance of science, the actual brewing process for draught Guinness has remained virtually unchanged for more than 200 years.

By the 1920s, advertising was starting to come into its own, and in 1928 the company launched a series of posters and newspaper adverts extolling the virtues of its wondrous drink. Its first campaign focused on the wholesome nature of its product. Market research at that time suggested that the British public believed that Guinness was a nourishing drink. The campaign sought to capitalize on this and was launched with the slogan: "Guinness is good for you." A number of well-known artists and writers contributed images and words, including John Gilroy, Rex Whistler and Dorothy L. Sayers. To cope with growing demand, a new brewery was established at

Park Royal in London. But Guinness set its sights beyond its British neighbours.

(Concerned that it might be misconstrued as a serious health claim, the Advertising Standards Authority later requested that the company withdraw the slogan. By then, however, Guinness had developed a taste for innovative advertising. The company introduced its first TV campaign in 1955, and in the 1960s the talking toucan was a precursor of beer advertising to come.)

To manage export activities, Guinness Exports Limited (GEL) was established after World War II, and in 1963 Guinness Overseas Limited was created to oversee the setting up of new Guinness breweries in foreign countries including Ghana, Nigeria, Malaysia and Cameroon. In the USA, the Guinness-Harp Corporation was established in the mid-1960s and became the Guinness Import Company in 1985.

In the 1980s, the good name of Guinness was blackened by a scandal over illegal attempts to support its share price during the attempted take-over of the Distillers company. Ernest Saunders, Guinness CEO at the time, was jailed for his involvement. His early release on medical grounds, and subsequent recovery, caused more unwanted publicity. However, this appears to have done surprisingly little damage to the Guinness brand.

For many years, however, despite its scientific approach, one goal evaded the company. Its reputation was built on the quality and taste of draught Guinness – a flavor that many said could not be transported in cans (some Guinness drinkers said it didn't travel beyond Dublin).

A take-home format was the logical next development. But putting Guinness draught in a can for home consumption proved problematic. The recreation of the famous creamy head, in particular, proved a stumbling block. The breakthrough came after four-year development project led by Dr Alan Forage, which created the ICS (in-can system) that mirrored the surge system used to pull pints of draught Guinness in pubs. The new product was successfully launched in the UK in 1989.

Over the years, too, the idea that drinking Guinness has nutritional benefits has persisted. Among them, that it is beneficial to pregnant women and patients suffering from anaemia. It has been enjoyed as an alcoholic tonic for years. This popular image is something played on by later Guinness advertising campaigns.

"Guinness for Strength" was a thematic development of the original "Guinness is good for you" campaign, intended to give the drink a more masculine image. The campaign was also a gentle send-up of the premise underlying most advertising – that buying a product can transform the user into a "better" person: more attractive, sexually desirable, socially popular and powerful.

The inherent humour was achieved by simple exaggeration; after supping a Guinness, you could apparently lift huge metal girders, pull a horse along in a cart or chop down a tree with the single blow of an axe. The "Pure Genius" campaign, started in 1986, introduced the actor Rutger Hauer as the "enigmatic man" and built on the mysterious, dark character of the product. The campaign was particularly appealing to a younger group of beer drinkers tired of the unsubtle messages of other beer commercials.

Guinness is less well known in North America. But in parts of the USA brand awareness is growing. Guinness Import Co., one commentator observed, "has built US marketing as one pours a pint of the black brew: slowly." As one senior executive at the company acknowledged: "In some ways the brand is a little mysterious, because it's acknowledged that it's not for everyone. We had to do some ground work to raise the level of awareness."

Before launching a major TV advertising campaign, Guinness prepared the ground by spending five years improving distribution. After complaints from consumers about the taste, the importer also sent out field teams to instruct American bars on the proper way to pour and serve Guinness draft, which uses a combination of nitrogen and carbon dioxide in its taps.

Britain's Guinness merged with Grand Metropolitan in 1997. The $22.3 billion deal created the company Diageo, and resulted in a brand marriage that brought the famous stout and Gordon's Gin under the same roof as Grand Met's J&B Scotch and Smirnoff vodka, with Burger King and Håagen-Dazs ice cream.

Brand magnets

Some companies have assembled formidable legions of big brand names.

Procter & Gamble

- Ariel
- Bounce
- Daz
- Dreft
- Fairy
- Lenor
- Flash
- Pampers
- Tampax
- Pringles
- Sunny Delight
- Crest
- Vicks
- Clearasil
- Cover Girl
- Max Factor
- Old Spice
- Hugo Boss
- Head & Shoulders
- Pantene Pro-V
- Vidal Sassoon
- Camay

Unilever

- Persil
- Radion
- Surf
- Comfort
- Domestos
- Jif
- Vim
- Dove
- Knight's
- Castile
- Lifebuoy
- Lux
- PearsPond's
- Vaseline
- Calvin Klein Cosmetics
- Obsession
- Elizabeth Arden
- Elizabeth Taylor Black Pearls
- Karl Lagerfeld
- KL
- Lagerfeld for Men
- Valentino
- Lynx
- Brut
- Faberge
- Impulse
- Organics hair care
- Salon Selectives
- Timotei

Unilever (cont'd)
- Signal
- Clearblue One Step
- Persona
- Flora
- I Can't Believe It's Not Butter!
- Bertolli
- Dante
- Boursin
- Brooke Bond PG Tips
- Lipton

- Cornetto
- Feast
- Magnum
- Viennetta
- Chicken Tonight
- Colman's
- Oxo
- Ragu
- Peperami
- Bird's Eye
- Walls

Nestlé
- Nescafé
- Perrier
- Contrex
- Vittel
- Valvert
- Buxton
- San Pellegrino
- Nesquick
- Nescau
- Carnation
- Libby's
- Coffee-mate
- Maggi
- Crosse & Blackwell
- Thorny
- Buitoni

- Contadina
- Findus
- Milkybar
- Kit Kat
- Quality Street
- Smarties
- Baci
- After Eight
- Lion
- Rolo
- Aero
- Polo
- Friskies
- L'Oréal (major shareholding)

Bass
- Carling
- Caffreys
- Worthingtons
- Hooper's Hooch
- Grolsch
- Tennents

- Britvic Soft Drinks
- Holiday Inn
- Inter-Continental Hotels
- All Bar One
- Edward's

Diageo
- Baileys
- Bells
- Burger King (UK)
- Cinzano
- Croft
- Crossbow Cider
- Dom Perignon
- Gilbey's Gin
- Gordon's Gin
- Green Giant
- Guinness
- Häagen-Dazs
- Haig Whisky
- Hennessy Cognac
- Kilkenny
- Johnnie Walker
- J&B
- Malibu

- Moët & Chandon
- Pillsbury
- Pimm's
- Red Stripe
- Skol
- Smirnoff
- Tanqueray Gin
- VAT 69
- Veuve Clicquot
- CPC International
- Marmite
- Bovril
- Pot Noodle
- Ambrosia
- Hellmann's Mayonnaise
- Knorr
- Mazola

Whitbread
- Beefeater
- Pizza Hut
- Café Rouge
- Dome
- TGI Fridays

- Bella Pasta
- Costa Coffee
- Marriott Hotels
- David Lloyd Leisure Clubs
- Boddington's

Whitbread (cont'd)
- Murphy's
- Stella Artois
- Heineken
- Labatt
- Rolling Rock

- Brewer's Fayre
- Family Inn
- Hogshead pubs
- Travel Inn

Häagen-Dazs

H äagen-Dazs was one of the super brands of the 1980s. It was a time of niche products and luxury brands. The indulgent ice cream fitted the times perfectly. The advertisers added another ingredient that made it unstoppable: sex. The slogan "dedicated to pleasure" and variations rapidly gave the dreamy ice cream superbrand status.

TIME magazine described Häagen-Dazs as "the best ice cream in the world." But the brand virtually invented the premium ice cream market. Others soon followed. But to date Häagen-Dazs leads. Market research shows it to be the clear brand leader (bar own label brands).

Few brands in recent years have used marketing so effectively as the US ice cream producer. First, there was the exotic name, plucked from nowhere to add a Danish twist. Second came the carefully communicated brand promise: pure indulgence. Only the finest ingredients were used to produce what was always positioned as a luxury consumer product. Häagen-Dazs broke the rules by transforming a children's treat into a luxury indulgence for adults.

The ice cream brand always commanded a premium price, but somehow, far from putting consumers off, it seemed to appeal to their desire for excess. Everything about the brand, from its sensual advertising to the packaging, invited consumers to spoil themselves. Here was the ultimate in hedonistic pleasures. Sex and ice cream, together. It didn't get any better than this. No matter that they couldn't afford the best of everything, in one area of their lives, they could go all the way. Millions did just that.

Filling the pot

The Häagen-Dazs brand made its mouth-watering debut in 1961. It was produced by Reuben Mattus, a New York entrepreneur. His dream was to make the finest ice cream the world had ever tasted.

Mattus was no ice cream neophyte. As an eight-year old, he came to the USA from Poland in 1921 with his widowed mother. His mother sold lemon ices made from lemons squeezed by hand. (Ice and ice cream pops were made from freezing juices in test tubes.)

In 1932, under his direction, Senator Frozen Products Inc. was established in the Bronx. By the late-1950s, he had built it up into a successful firm, which sold, among other things, an ice cream called Ciro's through outlets such as drug and grocery stores. By the 1960s, Mattus could see that the future belonged to larger outlets. He wanted to distribute ice cream through the supermarkets that were springing up. With their superior refrigeration and wide appeal, he believed the bigger retail outlets offered a market for ice cream all year round.

However, his Ciro's brand was soon squeezed out by the large dairies, which picked up on the idea and offered the large retail chains incentive deals that Ciro's couldn't match.

Mattus wasn't so easily put off. He came up with another idea: a luxury brand of ice cream made from fresh cream, real fruit and natural ingredients – marketed through the use of imaginatively named flavors. Somewhat bizarrely a Danish-sounding name, he decided, was the perfect touch to differentiate his new brand from the competition.

The first three Häagen-Dazs flavors were basic – vanilla, chocolate and coffee were sold through New York delicatessens. The response was immediate. Within a few weeks other stores across America were placing orders for the new ice cream. Such was its success that by the 1970s sales of the new brand had eclipsed those of Ciro's, which was closed down.

Throughout the early 1970s, Häagen-Dazs sales increased even though the product had no formal advertising and only word-of-mouth endorsements. Remarkably, this was sufficient to increase product distribution to urban centers and college towns in the Northeast. People began to write from across the country asking how they could get Häagen-Dazs in their area. A few fanatics even volunteered to distribute the product themselves.

What happened next was a defining moment for the brand. It took the product from being simply an ice cream brand and made it a retail channel in its own right. Mattus' daughter came up with the idea of a "dipping store," an entire retail outlet devoted solely to the Häagen-Dazs brand. The first store was opened in Brooklyn and ushered in a new era for the brand. It was followed by more stores in cities right across the USA.

By 1982, the company was pushing into new markets. Expansion into Canada was a natural next step. This was followed by a partnership with a leading Japanese dairy, and by the end of the 1980s, the ice cream had crossed the Atlantic to the Old World, where Europeans greeted the sensuous advertising that announced its arrival with enthusiasm.

The mid-1980s were kind to Häagen-Dazs. It's appeal to the "me generation" was direct. The passion for self indulgence was all consuming, and consume it they did by the truck load. By the early 1990s, Häagen-Dazs had become the coolest new bedroom accessory on the market. Ads featuring beautiful semi-naked men and women dipping into the luxurious ice cream cartons adorned the pages of magazines, newspapers and bill boards. Meanwhile, behind the scenes control shifted.

In the 1980s ownership of Häagen-Dazs changed hands twice. In 1983, it was bought by the Pillsbury Group. Pillsbury itself was then acquired by Grand Metropolitan in 1989. The 1980s also saw the brand add new products including frozen yoghurt bars, ice cream stick bars and frozen cakes, and the highly successful Extråas range of ice cream containing bite-sized chunks of ingredients.

But the 1980s also marked the arrival of another luxury ice cream brand: Ben & Jerry's Homemade. The story of the company founded by Ben Cohen and Jerry Greenfield, in an abandoned Vermont gas station, is well known. Their alternative ice cream empire competes directly with Häagen-Dazs.

What Ben & Jerry's brought to the market was luxury ice cream with hippy attitudes. In some respects, it was the next thing. After the pure hedonism of the 1980s, the baby boomer generation was attracted to frozen desserts with a moral message. Calorie concerns could wait, the new ice cream addicts felt, but saving the world couldn't. Ben & Jerry's full fat fudge sundaes with Utopian business values on top was seductive. Their hippy humor – with flavors such as Cherry Garcia (inspired by the leader of the Grateful Dead) also appealed.

Häagen-Dazs found itself on the defensive. The two companies had a series of highly publicized brushes involving legal action against the larger brand over attempts to prevent Ben & Jerry's from using the same distributors.

Like The Body Shop, however, Ben & Jerry's sends out mixed messages. Running a values-led business has sometimes got them tangled up in their own good intentions. Social change and full-fat ice cream can make odd bedfellows. The Häagen-Dazs message – full fat ice cream to be eaten with bedfellows – is a more seductive one.

The ice cream dream

- 1921: Reuben Mattus' family enters ices and ice cream business in the Bronx, New York. The eight-year-old Mattus comes to the USA from Poland in 1921 with his widowed mother. His mother sells lemon ices made from lemons squeezed by hand. Ice and ice cream pops are made from freezing juices in test tubes.
- 1932: Under Reuben Mattus' direction, Senator Frozen Products, Inc. is established.
- 1940s: Ice cream becomes a year-round treat due to technological advances in refrigeration. Mattus and wife, Rose, expand product line: product is sold under name of Ciro's.
- 1950s: Mattus' innovations change American ice cream industry. He is first to:
  - package ice cream in special low, round pint containers in New York;
  - color-key packaging to correspond with flavors;

- penetrate grocery store chains as year-round distribution for ice cream, providing them with freezer cabinets.

Mattus' innovations are copied by large dairy conglomerates which, through cost cutting, threaten existence of his family business. He realizes he has to find a niche; that niche becomes Häagen-Dazs.

- 1961: Häagen-Dazs name is registered. Product initially sold in expensive New York gourmet shops.
- 1960s through early 1970s: Häagen-Dazs sales increase as word-of-mouth creates demand for product.
- Mid-1970s: Doris Mattus Hurley, daughter of Reuben Mattus opens a "dipping store" in Brooklyn, New York. (By 1990, there are 250 Häagen-Dazs Shops throughout the USA. International locations include the UK, France, Germany, Singapore, Hong Kong and Japan.)
- 1978: Company moves Bronx plant (now a distribution depot for metro New York) to a larger facility in Woodbridge, New Jersey, capable of producing 20 million gallons of ice cream annually.
- 1980s: Begin globalization of the Häagen-Dazs brand.
- 1983: Häagen-Dazs purchased by the Pillsbury Company.
- 1984: Company signs agreement with Suntory, one of Japan's leading companies, and Takanashi, a leading Japanese dairy, to produce and sell Häagen-Dazs in Japan.
- 1985: A second Häagen-Dazs facility opens in Tulare, in the heart of California's dairy, fruit and nut country, for product distribution on the West Coast.
- 1989: Pillsbury bought by Grand Metropolitan.
- 1991: Häagen-Dazs introduces Frozen Yogurt in five flavors: Vanilla, Chocolate, Strawberry, Peach, and Vanilla.
- 1997: Grand Metropolitan merges with Guinness to create Diageo.

Harley-Davidson

T he essence of the Harley-Davidson brand can be summed up in one word: freedom. More than any other brand, the Milwaukee-based motorcycle company has come to stand for American individualism. Like other icon status brands, the company has come to realize that its greatest asset is a romanticized version of its past.

The Harley-Davidson brand heritage is part based on reality and part based on films such as *The Wild Bunch* and *Easy Rider*. It helps, too, that many of Hollywood's leading men – and one or two leading women – choose to own a Harley. Clever use of the brand has also allowed the company to move into merchandising, selling everything from Harley-Davidson clothes to deodorant and soft furnishings.

Today, the average age of a Harley customer is 42, compared to 32 ten years ago. The brand is benefiting from a new breed of professionals – accountants and lawyers who don motorcycle leathers at the weekend in search of freedom and another life away from the office. (Customers buying their first motorcycle or coming back to riding after a lapse increased more than three-fold between 1987 and 1994). Orders outstrip production creating a waiting list for many models. Year-old Harleys sell for 25 percent more than the list price of brand new ones.[1]

In 1997, the company enjoyed record sales of $1.75 billion, on 132,000 motorcycles, and commanded a hefty 48 percent share of the North American market for heavy road bikes (which is showing healthy growth of between eight and ten percent a year).

Born to be wild

In Milwaukee at the turn of the century, a young man called William Harley, 21, and his friend Arthur Davidson, 20, began experiments on "taking the work out of bicycling." They were joined by Arthur's brothers, Walter and William.

Many changes were made to the engine design before its builders were satisfied (the familiar 45 degree V-twin wasn't introduced until 1909). With the design of the looped frame, they began production in 1903.

Harley-Davidson erected its first building at the current Juneau Avenue site in 1906 and was incorporated in 1907. The total output that year was 150 motorcycles. By the time the famous V-twin went into production two years later the company was cranking out more than 1100 motorcycles a year.

Harley dominated racing events in the US, and its motorcycles were used by the American military, having proven their worth in border skirmishes with Pancho Villa. By the 1920s, Harley-Davidson had become the largest motorcycle manufacturer in the world and was exporting to dealers in 67 countries.

The roaring twenties brought many of the innovations that became Harley trademarks, including the tear drop petrol tank and the novel addition of a front brake. The Wall Street Crash took its toll on motorcycle sales, but the company bounced back with the introduction of its EL model – known as the "Knucklehead."

America's entry into World War II saw the entire Harley production dispatched to the military. After the war, the company celebrated its 50th anniversary as its oldest and closest rival, Indian, closed its doors.

Harley introduced the Sportster in 1957. In 1958, Carroll Resweber won the first of four consecutive AMA Grand National Championships on a Harley. In the same year, the Duo Glide went into production – with the addition of an electric starter, this became the Electra Glide in 1965.

The company went public in 1965 and took a new turn four years later when it merged with the American Foundry Company (AMF). In 1971, the company introduced the Super Glide, another landmark model. The arrival of the Tour Glide – dubbed "King of the Highway" – marked Harley's entry into the market for touring motorcycles.

In 1981, a group of 13 senior Harley executives led by Vaughn Beals bought the company. They celebrated with a victory ride from the company's factory in York, Pennsylvania, to its headquarters in Milwaukee. The new owners started the Harley Owners Group (HOG) to get customers more involved with the brand.

In 1983, tariffs were imposed on Japanese motorcycles of 700 cc and above, and Harley unveiled its new – more reliable – 1340 cc V2 Evolution engine.

In July 1987, Harley-Davidson received a listing on the New York Stock Exchange. In 1993, the company celebrated its 90th anniversary with more than 100,000 Harley enthusiasts converging on Milwaukee and a drive through parade featuring 60,000 Harley-Davidson machines.

Brand cruising

The story appears to be one of a brand operating on cruise control. When CEO Richard Teerlink climbed into the saddle at Harley-Davidson in 1989, he inherited one of the strongest brand images in the world. Brand loyalty among dedicated Harley enthusiasts remained unshakeable, but the company was on the slide. Quality had become an issue as the famous brand tried to get costs down to compete with aggressive Japanese incursions. To add insult to injury, the Japanese were stealing a slice of the market for cruising factory custom bikes with machines modeled on the Harley blueprint.

Teerlink knew things had to change. He keyed into Harley's greatest asset – the people who care about the Harley-Davidson brand. He opened a dialog outside the company with the loyal customer base and inside the company with its workforce. As a result, the Harley Owners Group has 325,000 members. This number is likely to grow: Harley hopes to increase production from 118,000 in 1996 to between 200,000 and 300,000 by the company's centenary in 2003.

Teerlink also introduced a rigorous new build quality regime to ensure that what left the factory was worthy of the Harley-Davidson name. This meant that customers sometimes had to wait to take delivery of their new motorcycles, but guaranteed the machine they received would be worth the wait.

Management processes were also overhauled. They are now benchmarks of fashionable best practice. For example, Harley uses self-directed teams at executive level. It eliminated executive vice presidents from its hierarchy and, instead, created three linked teams. The teams reflect the way the company is organized. One is responsible for creating demand, another for producing products and the final one for support.[2]

Organizational changes have been backed by investments in training. The company has the Harley Institute, which focuses on key competencies (divided into interaction, execution and technical). All employees receive 80 hours of training every year and dealers are now offered a three-day training program.

These and other initiatives paved the way for the remarkable comeback of Harley-Davidson in the 1990s. In 1995, Harley introduced the Heritage Springer Softail, laying claim to the future with its own special branding of the past. Today, however, other heritage names are re-appearing, including the British motorcycle legend Triumph. New brands are also tapping into the old ways.

Victory and Excelsior-Henderson are the most ambitious of a group of homegrown US start-up motorcycle companies. Generating unparalleled customer loyalty and dedication, the torque of the Harley-Davidson brand, however, should be sufficient to see off the new pretenders for many years to come.

Notes

1   Schonfeld, Erick, "Betting on the Boomers," *Fortune*, 1995.
2   Imperato, Gina, "Harley shifts gear," *Fast Company*, Issue 9, June/July 1997.

Harvard Business School

Harvard Business School is the premier brand in business education. It is a brand that allows the business school to charge premium prices for everything it does.

Today, the HBS brand covers a surprisingly wide range of activities. These include academic qualification courses such as the MBA (Master of Business Administration); executive education programs companies send their top managers on; and a publishing operation responsible for the *Harvard Business Review* and business books. As befits its inventor, the HBS is also a prodigious producer of branded case studies which are used at management education institutions all over the world.

Its greatest strength lies in its ability to leverage intellectual capital. In business school terminology the HBS brand has synergy. The Harvard logo can facilitate a seamless roll-out – even provide a launch pad for an entire mini-industry. An idea that starts out as an article in the *Harvard Business Review* can be developed into a book, then a video or CD-ROM. On the back of the book, the successful author joins the international conference circuit, thereby generating still more sales.

For some, it is the perfect virtuous circle. Flushed with success, the wandering business professor eventually returns to the welcoming arms of HBS where the original idea is developed into exciting new courses, and attracts funding for further research which sets the whole cycle in motion once more. With the HBS brand, there is no need to worry about product life cycle.

As a result of its association with Harvard Business School, HBS Publishing has access not only to the latest thinking on management but also to the latest management thinkers – many of whom are guru brands in their own right.

Several of its most prominent authors are HBS faculty members, including the school's dean Kim Clark, Linda Hill, Rosabeth

Moss Kanter, Robert Kaplan, John Kotter and Michael Porter. The company also publishes the work of some of the biggest selling management writers including Arie de Geus; Gary Hamel; Charles Handy; Regis McKenna, and C.K. Prahalad. Several are affiliated to other business schools, but are pleased to be published under the Harvard brand.

Planting the ivy

Harvard Business School was founded in 1908, and awarded its first Masters degree in management in 1910. Although other schools – notably the Tuck School at Dartmouth – claim to have had graduate programs in management before that date, HBS was the first business school to require a university degree for entry to its management program.

What the school also had that set it apart from many of the other business schools springing up in America at that time was the Harvard brand. The combination of the Ivy League prestige of Harvard University, the serious approach the new school took to the fledgling discipline of management, and its ability to attract gifted professors – some of them from other parts of the university, soon established the school as the top institution of its kind.

Wallace Dohan, dean of Harvard Business School, oversaw the 1922 launch of the *Harvard Business Review*. "The effect of hedging upon flour mill control" hardly set the pulse racing, but was the beginning of a publishing success story and a prestigious addition to the Harvard brand. For more than 75 years the *Harvard Business Review* has been influential in shaping management thinking around the globe. Today, along with reprints of articles from the HBR archive, busy executives can buy audio tapes of articles to listen to in their cars or on long flights.

HBS benefited from the MBA boom. While the qualification cemented its place during the 1960s and 1970s, its apotheosis came in the 1980s. Suddenly it seemed that recruiters couldn't get enough of the newly minted business school graduates. The investment banks and management consultancies that had always valued the analytical skills provided by the MBA were joined by blue-chip companies from other sectors.

With a flourish, the MBA seemed to epitomize the free market philosophy that dominated Western democracies during that decade. Thatcher and Reagan's children were bottle-fed on the enterprise culture. Suddenly, commerce in all its guises was not just a respectable activity, but a moral imperative.

The MBA *was* the 1980s as much as Gordon Gekko or *The Bonfire of the Vanities*. Masters of the Universe, in Tom Wolfe's phrase, came armed with an MBA. It was part of the *zeitgeist*. The spirit of the decade was well-heeled young managers stepping straight out of business school into high-powered executive jobs. Simply having the three letters after your name was believed to be enough to add a zero to your salary. Never before or since has a qualification been so lucrative – or so hyped. Stories about the "golden hellos" – joining bonuses – on offer to MBA graduates at the time abounded. Especially popular with business graduates joining investment banks on Wall Street and in the City of London, and those going into the leading management consultancies, they became part of the mythology of the MBA.

At the top of the pile was the Harvard branded MBA.

The HBS brand is also a big draw in the executive education market. Companies happily fork out $40,500 to send executives on the prestigious nine-week Advanced Management Program at Harvard.

The case study industry is also booming, despite some concerns that the case study method provides a superficial view of running a business. Traditionally, the case study has been one of the educational building blocks of MBA programs throughout the world. It was established as the primary method of teaching at Harvard Business School as long ago as 1924. Case studies present students with a corporate example. From the narrative, they are expected to reach conclusions about what was the right or wrong thing to do, identify best and worst practice, and learn something about managerial behavior. Harvard alone has generated 5310 cases – although one on the use of the Harvard brand has yet to be published. The case study method remains a globally accepted and practised approach.

Harvard continues to churn out around 600 cases a year (as well as around 40 books). In recent years, HBS branding has gone high-tech, creating CD-ROM, audio and video formats for many of its products. It is now possible to pay for HBR articles on-line and down load them instantly. Even the traditional case study has taken a digital turn. Harvard put its first electronic case to work in 1996 and now boasts that its MBA curriculum is "virtually paperless" with an expanding number of electronic cases incorporating on-site video sequences and links to real-time information on the Internet.

Harvard's influence stretches around the world. The Indian Institute of Management, for example, was established with Harvard's support and remains a devout follower to this day. A number of European business schools also followed the Harvard model, including IESE, the prestigious Spanish school. In Asia, the Manila-based Asian Institute of Management was launched in 1968 and, initially used material from Harvard for all of its programs. (Harvard even offers a one-year program in applied economics with the Ho Chi Minh City Economics University in Vietnam thus achieving by stealth what the US failed to achieve through warfare.)

Not everyone is convinced that HBS delivers on its brand promise to create better business leaders, however. The brand has also picked up one or two negative endorsements. Peter Drucker has roundly dismissed Harvard – "Harvard, to me, combines the worst of German academic arrogance with bad American theological seminary habits," he has observed.

Still more opinionated was the late Avis chief and author of *Up the Organization*, Robert Townsend. "Don't hire Harvard Business School graduates," he warned. "This elite, in my opinion, is missing some pretty fundamental requirements for success: humility; respect for people in the firing line; deep understanding of the nature of the business and the kind of people who can enjoy themselves making it prosper; respect from way down the line; a demonstrated record of guts, industry, loyalty down, judgment, fairness, and honesty under pressure."

But the critics are in the minority. With the executive education market looking set to carry on growing, the HBS brand is well placed to take maximum advantage. If the brand has an Achilles Heel it lies in its intellectual arrogance. To date it has shown itself to be an adequate if not a spectacular innovator. As the competition increases, it will have to pick up its feet or risk being overtaken by more agile business school brands.

H eineken has been refreshing the parts other beers cannot reach for more than 130 years. In the seemingly homogenous lager market, the Dutch beer uses a quirky sense of humor and strong brand personality to stand out from the crowd. Today, it is one of the best selling beer brands in the world, second only to Budweiser.

In the 1970s and 1980s the company used a highly effective advertising campaign to break into the British market, which had traditionally been dominated by domestic ales and bitters. The Heineken ads concentrated on the notion of refreshment. Pilsner lager was served cold. At the same time, it made much of its continental European heritage. Above all, though, the campaign was designed to appeal to young people. It was irreverent, slightly risqué, and in complete contrast to the fusty, working class image of the domestic beers. Drinking Heineken was fun.

The commercials made a series of outrageous claims about the refreshing qualities of Heineken beer. It was the remedy for everything from tired feet to bad piano playing. In the first ten years of the campaign, sales in Britain increased by 300 percent, despite the arrival of more than 100 other lagers on British shores.

Between 1974 and 1985, Heineken commercials went on to give a lift to Mr Spock's ears, bring a ruddy glow back to Rudolph's red nose, and turn arch villain J.R. Ewing into an angel complete with halo. Such was the power of the campaign that it became part of everyday language and inspired the humor of comedians.

The brewing of a brand

The Heineken story began in 1863 when Gerard Adriaan Heineken bought the De Hooiberg brewery, the largest brewery in Amsterdam.

The business went from strength to strength with Heineken opening new breweries in Amsterdam and Rotterdam.

In search of quality ingredients and the latest brewing technology, Heineken toured Europe. In Germany he was quick to spot the move from the traditional top-fermenting method to bottom fermentation. Heineken hired a German as brewmaster of his beer. Later innovations involved the development of new recipes. Then in 1886, one Dr Elion, a former student at Louis Pasteur's school, developed the famous "Heineken A yeast" – which still gives the beer its distinctive flavor.

By the time Heineken died in 1893, his brewing business had become one of the most important in Holland. But competition from other Dutch beers – including Amstel – and German rivals forced the company to cut the price of its beer. The depression of the 1930s brought more competition and a decline in the consumption of beer across Europe. After Holland was liberated, the Heineken management faced an uphill battle to rebuild its brewing empire.

European sales increased steadily over the next two decades. But the Dutch beer struggled to break into the British market, where traditional ales and bitters were still more popular than continental style lagers. The "tied house" system of pubs, and a tax duty that penalized stronger brews made it difficult for a traditional pilsner lager to compete.

In 1951, Heineken introduced a specially adapted – weaker – lager for the UK market. This marked a radical departure for Heineken, which had always insisted its unique flavour should not be compromised to suit local tastes. Despite this accommodation, however, sales in the UK remained disappointing until the 1970s when lager became more widely drunk. In 1985, the company introduced "Heineken Special Export," which in accordance with Heineken's positioning in other international markets is promoted and priced as a premium beer.

In the US market, however, Heineken fared better. Heineken was the first foreign brewery to export beer to America after Prohibition was lifted. Americans were used to domestic beers based on the continental lager model and enjoyed the heritage of the Heineken

Pilsner. Its premium pricing and quality branding worked like a charm and quickly made it America's favourite imported beer.

Reaching the markets other beers cannot reach

Heineken has always insisted that its core values are centered around the quality of its product and its ability to penetrate overseas markets. With an increase in premium lager market forecast, and the growth of designer beers, micro-brewers and technological innovations including dry beers, lite beers and ice beers the competition looks set to intensify.

Despite the advantage of high brand recognition, it is unclear whether Heineken is equipped to meet these challenges. Unlike many of the leading domestic beers, Heineken's brand loyalty with American beer drinkers has not proved particularly strong. It appears to enjoy the "best of the imports" slot in many consumers' minds. The danger is that with other premium imports increasingly available it could lose its premium brand price appeal.

In Britain and some other European markets, Heineken became a victim of fashion. In the 1980s, the influx of US and Australian beers made a big impact not because they offered anything substantially different, but because they seemed more in tune with the times. The New World was perceived as more exciting than the old world of which Heineken and other continental beers were a part. Some brands – Skol and Harp, for example – were hit especially hard. But the onslaught also took its toll on quality brands such as Heineken.

Today's beer drinkers are even less loyal to brands. Though less consciously influenced by fashion, they are much more likely to try different beers in the constant search to assert their individuality. This may be good news for micro brewers but for mass market brands like Heineken, it is less welcome. What will stand the Dutch beer in good stead in the coming years is its sense of fun and brand personality that allows it to adapt to changing market conditions.

Heinz

enry John Heinz (1844–1916) was born in Pittsburgh. He was a precocious entrepreneur – at the age of eight (or twelve depending on which history book you read) he was selling surplus home grown vegetables. This quickly mushroomed into an empire. By 1860, he was delivering three wagons full of vegetables to Pittsburgh grocers every week.

Heinz's business continued to grow and in 1869 he went into a partnership selling, of all things, grated horseradish. The horseradish was notable for its purity – Henry wasn't tempted to add turnip as others did. This was demonstrated by the use of a clear jar. This proved a salutary experience: the partnership went bankrupt six years later. The failure was caused by a surfeit of crops, which lowered prices. (Typically, Heinz paid off all his creditors.) Undaunted, Heinz bounced back and launched F & J Heinz with his brother and cousin as partners, and himself as the manager, in 1876. The new company made pickles and condiments. One of its first products was tomato ketchup.

Henry Heinz had bold ambitions. "Our market is the world," he proclaimed with customary gusto. In search of new markets, he visited Europe. Famously, he turned up at London's prestigious Fortnum & Mason store with five cases of goods. After tasting the samples, the Fortnum & Mason purchaser is reputed to have said: "I think, Mr Heinz, we will take the lot." By 1900, Heinz salesmen were selling the company's range of 200 products throughout the world. It was claimed that they visited "every inhabited continent."

In 1888 the company was re-established as HJ Heinz and, in 1892, Henry Heinz decided the company needed a slogan. He came up with "57 varieties" to describe the foods sold by the company. This was one of the few cases of successful under-selling – Heinz produced 60 products at the time – but one that has stood the test of time. Heinz was a born marketer. "It's not so much what you say but how, when and where," he sagely observed.

His company was incorporated in 1905 with Henry as president. Heinz's business philosophy was straight out of the Victorian philanthropist's guide book. "Heart power is better than horse power," he said. His factory by the Allegheny River was something of a model for the way in which people were treated and its cleanliness. Heinz instigated factory tours to show of the factory to interested parties. At the time of his death in 1916, the company employed thousands of people at 25 factories.

Beyond Henry

Henry Heinz was succeeded by his son, Howard. Howard Heinz moved the company into baby food and prepared soups – when Allied troops landed in Normandy in 1944 they carried self-heating cans of Heinz soup. Later, Henry's grandson, Jack Heinz, took control. He continued the company's faith in advertising and promotion. Its wartime slogans included the memorable "Beans to bombers" and "Pickles to pursuit planes."

It was not until 1965, when R. Burt Gookin became CEO, that the Heinz family relinquished control of the top job. Gookin was followed by former Irish rugby international Tony O'Reilly. Some things didn't change. "My acid test ... is whether a housewife, intending to buy Heinz tomato ketchup in a store, finding it to be out of stock, will walk out of the store to buy it elsewhere or switch to an alternative product," says Tony O'Reilly.[1]

Along the way, Heinz acquired StarKist (1963); Ore-Ida (1965) and Weight Watchers International (1978). Heinz is now on only its sixth CEO – William R. Johnson took on the top job in 1998. Johnson champions an equation for success called V5V – "Heinz will achieve success through the 5 Vs: a vision based on global category management and growth; a voracious appetite for success; an unyielding focus on enhancing shareholder value; a dedication to volume growth fueled by cost containment; and a high velocity commitment to change."

The contemporary Heinz company has a market capitalization of $18.5 billion; over 40,000 employees and markets more than 5,000 varieties in over 200 countries.

Bean counting

- 1869: Henry J. Heinz and Clarence Noble launch Heinz & Noble.
- 1876: Tomato ketchup Heinz style is added to the product range.
- 1896: "57 Varieties" slogan coined.
- 1931: Howard Heinz moves the company into baby food and soups.
- 1946: Jack Heinz leads the company into public ownership.
- 1966: R. Burt Gookin becomes first non-family CEO.
- 1979: Tony O'Reilly becomes CEO and ignites global expansion.
- 1998: William R. Johnson becomes sixth Heinz CEO.

The rise of private labels

The development of food brands reveals many of the important stages in the development of brands as a whole. The origins of some of the world's largest food brands lie in the nineteenth century when the likes of Heinz and Nestlé created a vast new market in mass-produced food.

Having invented the market, the companies realized that its parameters were increasingly evident. In response to the simple fact that there's a limit to how much people can eat, the companies shifted their attention to value-added products to which they could attach premium prices. The emphasis was on pre-packed meals, eating healthily, speed and efficiency. A myriad of different brands and segments emerged. Consumers wanted to eat tasty, healthy food. They wanted it pre-prepared, ready and easy to cook.

The result was a massive market. By the 1990s one estimate put the global sales of packaged food at $2.8 trillion. Huge profits and cash reserves meant that the companies could afford to buy brands from other areas of the foods business. In the 1980s there was a steady stream of mergers and acquisitions. Enormous amounts of money and huge numbers of brands changed hands.

As is always the case, even in the world of booming brand budgets, reality returns. As premium prices increased, budgets mushroomed and the value of brands headed towards the commercial stratosphere, but consumers began to become a little reticent. They looked elsewhere and began to concentrate on value for money and the hard facts beyond the marketing.

Supermarkets quickly moved to take advantage of this change in emphasis through developing their own brands which had grown, but not hugely, in the last decades. From having a 23 percent share of packaged grocery turnover in 1978, own-label goods rose to 34.9 percent in 1991. Indeed, research by the Henley Center found that "best" brands are now often retailer's own-brands. The leading Dutch supermarket chain Albert Heijn's own-label products were ranked far ahead of Nestlé on all criteria – including trustworthiness, product innovation and packaging as well as price. The wheel has turned full circle. Indeed, some retail chains are now buying directly from farmers in another effort to increase profit margins. In doing so, they are simply repeating what Henry Heinz did when he was a boy entrepreneur.

Notes

1   Kotler, Philip, *Marketing Management*, Prentice Hall, Englewood
    Cliffs, NJ, 1996.

Hertz Car-Hire

Hertz is the leading brand in the car-rental industry. The company is as much a part of the American automobile story as the manufacturers in Detroit. From its pioneering founder Walter L. Jacobs, who started by renting out a dozen Model T Fords from a back street car lot in Chicago, through a spate of acquisitions and mergers, including ownership by the Ford Motor Company in the 1990s, to the present day, Hertz has remained the car-rental brand in front.

The company celebrated its 80th anniversary with the announcement of record sales. It's reputation for excellent service and its blanket coverage of North America and other parts of the world have made Hertz the first choice for millions of travellers. The company has always prided itself on being an innovator in its industry. As early as 1926, the company introduced a vital merchandizing idea in car-rental – the credit card – at the industry's first national convention. The National Credential card as it was called, was a forerunner of the Hertz International AUTO-matic charge card, introduced in 1959.

Other Hertz firsts have made it easier for rental customers to find their way to their destinations. Introduced to Hertz outlets in 1984, for example, the Computerized Driving Directions (CDD) provide customers with detailed directions to local destinations – available in six languages. Its long-time rival Avis may "try harder," but it is attention to customer needs that has kept the Hertz brand ahead of the pack.

Driving the brand

The company that became Hertz started renting automobiles in 1918. The business was started by Walter L. Jacobs, a pioneer of the auto rental sector. Aged 22, Jacobs opened a car-rental operation in Chicago. His original rental fleet was a dozen Model T Fords which he repaired and repainted himself.

By 1923, the business had grown, generating annual revenues of about $1 million. That same year Jacobs sold his car-rental business to John Hertz, president of the Yellow Cab and Yellow Truck and Coach Manufacturing Company. Jacobs remained with the company, as Hertz's senior executive.

The business was renamed the Hertz Drive U-Self System, and in 1926 became part of General Motors Corporation when GM acquired Yellow Truck from John Hertz.

In 1953, the Hertz businesses were bought from GM by the Omnibus Corporation, which got rid of the bus operation and concentrated on car and truck rental. In 1954, it became the Hertz Corporation and was listed on the New York Stock Market for the first time. Jacobs, the founder of the original rental business, became the company's first president and remained in the post until his retirement in 1960. He died in 1985 at the age of 88, leaving behind the most successful car rental brand in the world.

In 1954, Hertz acquired Metropolitan Distributors, a New York truck leasing operation dating back to World War I. In the process it also acquired Leon C. Greenbaum, who was head of Metropolitan. Greenbaum earned a place on the Hertz board and subsequently became chairman before his appointment in 1960 as CEO.

In the next two decades Hertz changed hands three more times. In 1967, it became a wholly owned subsidiary of RCA Corporation. Then in 1985, it joined UAL Inc., before being sold on December 30, 1987 to Park Ridge Corporation, a company formed by Ford Motor Company and Hertz management for the purpose of buying Hertz, and which in 1988 gave its name to the new Hertz headquarters Park Ridge, New Jersey.

The 1980s saw a flurry of activity in the car-rental sector with manufacturers keen to drive away their own rental business. Between them, Detroit's Big Three automakers General Motors, Ford and Chrysler bought up many of the big rental franchises. Already part-owned by Ford, Hertz, the leading brand in its market, was unlikely to escape their attentions for long.

In 1988, Volvo North America Corporation also became an investor in Park Ridge. Then in 1993, Park Ridge was merged into the Hertz Corporation and Hertz became an independent, wholly owned subsidiary of Ford.

The contemporary brand

By the mid-1990s, the car manufacturers were keen to trade in their rental interests. GM, which had owned National Car Rental System and a 29 percent stake in Avis, sold both. In January 1997, Ford agreed a deal to sell Budget Rent A Car to Team Rental Group Inc., its biggest franchiser, for $350 million. Others followed. Ford also announced that it would sell a 20 percent stake in Hertz, the biggest franchise with close to a quarter of a million vehicles in the U.S., in a public offering. The initial offering was made on 25 April 1997, at which time Hertz became a publicly listed company on the New York Stock Exchange.

Despite the uncertainty surrounding the sale, the brand performed well over the year, with a rise in income of 27 percent to $201.6 million, the fourth successive year of record earnings. 1997 was also a good year for awards; the business received 16 awards for service excellence and customer satisfaction, including the Conde Nast Traveller.

The Hertz brand has also been used successfully in the industrial equipment rental sector. In 1997, for example, Hertz Equipment Rental Corporation amounted to a $444.5 million business, operating from 135 locations across America and 13 European locations. Today, the brand is also used for a number of other business opportunities. These include insurance replacement rental, car sales, leasing, claim management and telecommunications.

In 1998, Hertz celebrated its 80th anniversary. With over 5500 outlets in the USA and a presence in some 140 other countries it had a worldwide purchased fleet of around half a million vehicles. Among the leading brand names, Hertz is the only one to exercise corporate control over its operations right across North America, Australia, New Zealand, Western Europe and Brazil.

"Y ou shouldn't gloat about anything you've done; you ought to keep going and try to find something better to do," said David Packard (1912–96), co-founder of the company which still bears his name. The brand is what you do; how you behave; how people see you behave.

Hewlett-Packard is akin to IBM in the 1960s: everyone's epitome of a well-managed company. As a brand, it is not universally loved or universally known or universally used. It is not particularly smart or brash. But, it is associated with excellence. Indeed, when they were assembling their list of "excellent" companies in the late 1970s, Tom Peters and Robert Waterman included Hewlett-Packard. It was one of their least controversial choices. Similarly, when Jerry Porras and James Collins wrote *Built to Last,* their celebration of long-lived companies, there was no doubt that Hewlett-Packard was worthy of inclusion. In 1985, *Fortune* ranked Hewlett-Packard as one of the two most highly admired companies in America. The company is ranked similarly in virtually every other poll on well-managed companies or ones which would be good to work for. The H-P brand has pulled off an unusual double: it is admired and successful.

Hewlett-Packard began in 1937 when, with a mere $538 and a rented garage in Palo Alto, Bill Hewlett and Packard set up in business. The two had met while students at nearby Stanford. Their ambitions were typical of many young people starting a business. "We thought we would have a job for ourselves. That's all we thought about in the beginning," said Packard. "We hadn't the slightest idea of building a big company." The garage was the birthplace of Silicon Valley.

In their first year of business Hewlett and Packard achieved sales of $5100 with $1300 in profits. Hewlett-Packard's first success was a device for measuring sound waves, which they sold to Walt Disney. An automatic lettuce thinner and a shock machine to help people lose weight followed. They also pondered on the market opportunities for automatic urinal flushers, bowling alley sensors and air conditioning equipment. The duo left the garage for good in 1940.

During wartime the business flourished, employing 144 people at its height. Immediately after the war, sales fell off – by half in 1946 alone. Undaunted, Hewlett and Packard hired technical talent. The business revived. By 1948, the company's sales were $2.1 million.

Their secret, said Hewlett and Packard, lay in the simplicity of their methods. "Professors of management are devastated when I say we were successful because we had no plans. We just took on odd jobs," said Hewlett. But their legacy is not the efficiency of their lettuce thinner or the quality of their urinal flusher, it lies in the culture of the company they created and the management style they used to run it, the H-P way.

Building from simplicity

From the very start, Hewlett-Packard worked to a few fundamental principles. It did not believe in long-term borrowing to secure the expansion of the business. Its recipe for growth was simply that its products needed to be leaders in their markets. It got on with the job. "Our main task is to design, develop and manufacture the finest [electronic equipment] for the advancement of science and the welfare of humanity. We intend to devote ourselves to that task," said Packard in a 1961 memo to employees.

The duo eschewed fashionable management theory. "If I hear anybody talking about how big their share of the market is or what they're trying to do to increase their share of the market, I'm going to personally see that a black mark gets put in their personnel folder," Packard said in a 1974 speech.

The company believed that people could be trusted and should always be treated with respect and dignity. "We both felt fundamentally that people want to do a good job. They just need guidelines on how to do it," said Packard.

H-P believed that management should be available and involved – Managing By Wandering About was the motto. Indeed, rather than the administrative suggestions of management, Packard preferred to talk of leadership.

If there was conflict, it had to be tackled through communication and consensus rather than confrontation. "Their legacy, and the achievement that Packard was most proud of, is a management style based on openness and respect for the individual," noted Louise Kehoe of the *Financial Times* in Packard's obituary.[1] Former CEO John Young has observed: "Our basic principles have endured intact since our founders conceived them. We distinguish between core values, and practices; the core values don't change, but the practices might."[2]

Hewlett-Packard was a company built on very simple ideas. While all about were turning into conglomerates, Hewlett and Packard kept their heads down and continued with their methods. When their divisions grew too big – and by that they meant around 1500 people – they split them up to ensure that they didn't spiral out of control.

They kept it simple. Nice guys built a nice company. They didn't do anything too risky or too outlandish. (Packard was skeptical about pocket calculators though, in the end, the company was an early entrant into the market.) They didn't bet the company on a big deal or get into debt. Indeed, in his research Richard Pascale identified "terminal niceness" as a potential problem for the company. Being criticized for being too good could only happen in the business world. For living up to their simple standards, Hewlett-Packard deserve acknowledgement.

Indeed, their values worked to save the company when times were hard. During the 1970s recession, Hewlett-Packard staff took a 10 percent pay cut and worked 10 percent less hours. If the company hadn't had a long-term commitment to employee stock ownership perhaps they wouldn't have been so keen to make sacrifices. The company also took advantage of lucky breaks which would have been missed elsewhere – in 1979 one of its engineers found that by heating metal in a specific way, it splattered all over. The decision to exploit this technology launched the ink jet printer business – ten years later, this decision became the basis for over $6 billion in H-P revenues.

On Packard's death in 1996, the company had 100,000 employees in 120 countries with revenues of $31 billion. It continues to move on. H-P chief Lew Platt has suggested that H-P should stand for "healthy paranoia" and explained why: "General Motors, Sears, International Business Machines, were the greatest companies in their industries, the best of the best in the world. These companies did not make gigantic mistakes. They were not led by stupid, inept people. The only real mistake they made was to keep doing what it was that had made them successful for a little too long."[3]

Notes

1 Kehoe, Louise, "Radical who built group with open management style," *Financial Times*, March 28, 1996.
2 Porras, Jerry, & Collins, James, *Built to Last*, Century, New York, 1994.
3 Kehoe, Louise, "Change while you are ahead," *Financial Times*, March 18, 1994.

*H*oliday *I*nn

In the Summer of 1951, the Wilson family of Memphis set off on a motoring vacation. There was nothing special about it. Just a couple and their five children heading to Washington, DC. Mr Wilson, Kemmons Wilson, was a Memphis builder and realtor. He and his family became exasperated as their vacation progressed. It was not a great deal of fun staying in expensive and poor quality motels.

"A motel room only cost about $8 a night, but the proprietors inevitably charged $2 extra for each child. So the $8 charge soon ballooned into an $18 charge for my family," Wilson later recounted. "If we could get a room with two beds, our two daughters slept in one, and Dorothy and I slept in the other. Our three boys slept on the floor in sleeping bags. Sometimes there was a dollar deposit for the key and another dollar for the use of a television."

So, Wilson (born 1913) decided to build his own – "I was seized by an idea: I could build a chain of affordable hotels, stretching from coast to coast. Families could travel cross-country and stay at one of my hotels every night." Wilson envisaged 400 such motels. It sounded outrageously ambitious, but Wilson didn't hang around. He began work while still on vacation. He measured rooms and looked at facilities. His conclusion was that features such as televisions, telephones, ice machines and restaurants should be universal. In his imagined hotel chain, children would be free.

When the family returned home, Wilson got straight to work. He asked a draftsman to draw up some plans. The draftsman had seen a Bing Crosby film the previous evening and labelled the plan, Holiday Inn, from the Crosby movie. Wilson liked it. The name stuck.

The first Holiday Inn was opened in Memphis in 1952. (This fared better than Wilson's first house, which he had mistakenly built on the wrong lot.) The rest is motel history. Clean and cheap, Holiday Inns spouted up throughout the USA and then the world. "He changed the way America travels," Senator John Glenn concluded of Wilson. "Kemmons Wilson has transformed the motel from the old wayside fleabag into the most popular home away from home," noted *TIME*. By the time Wilson retired in 1979, Holiday Inn was the world's largest lodging chain. Today there are 1643 Holiday Inn hotels with 327,059 rooms.

Half luck

After coming up with the idea and having launched the first Holiday Inn at 4985 Summer Avenue, Kemmons Wilson attempted to franchise the idea. Opening four Holiday Inns in just over a year in Memphis had stretched his finances to their limits. Twelve franchisers were sold to housebuilders for $500 each. Only three were eventually built. Wilson thought again and sold 120,000 shares at $9.75.

This provided the impetus necessary to create a nationwide chain. The 50th Holiday Inn was opened in 1958; the 100th in 1959; the 500th in 1964.

Wilson attributes his success to a combination of timing and sound business thinking – his autobiography is entitled *Half Luck, Half Brains*. Away from Holiday Inn, Kemmons Wilson has continued in his entrepreneurial way. In his late 60s, he put his fortune on the line to build Orange Lack Country Club in Kissimmee, Florida. It became the world's largest timeshare resort with nearly 60,000 owners. Kemmons Wilson companies ("Over 50 businesses ranging from pork rinds to candy," Wilson has said) now include Wilson Air Center; Wilson Hotel Management Company; Wilson-Todd Construction; and Wilson Graphics.

In 1979, Wilson gave control of Holiday Inns to his two sons. Since then, Holiday Inn has been controlled by a number of corporate names. Holiday Inn is now part of the large UK-based leisure and entertainment group, Bass, which is owner or franchiser of over 2600 Inter-Continental, Crowne Plaza, Holiday Inn, Holiday Inn Express and Staybridge Suites. Holiday Inn remains the most widely recognized lodging brand in the world. Bass is now building what it labels the "Holiday Inn of the Future." Kemmons Wilson is watching.

Hoover

The Hoover brand continues to rank among the top ten most widely recognized brands of products for the home. Hoover is one of a rare breed of brands that have become synonymous with the product category, earning it an entry in the Oxford dictionary. (The word Hoover is often used in place of vacuum cleaner and the verb "to hoover" – to clean with a vacuum cleaner.)

From its headquarters building at Main and East Maple streets in North Canton, Ohio, Hoover has provided vacuum cleaners to generations of Americans and families around the world. In terms of brand recognition, the Hoover brand enjoys top-of-mind brand awareness nearly four times greater than its nearest rival.

The early years

William H. Hoover was born in 1849, in Lancaster County, Pennsylvania. In 1875, Hoover purchased the John Lind tannery in present-day North Canton, Ohio, where he relocated his family and business. The company was eventually renamed The W.H. Hoover Company.

In 1907, Hoover, known as "The Boss," made a decision that would make the Hoover brand synonymous with the vacuum cleaner. His wife's cousin, Murray Spangler, was the night janitor at a Canton department store. An asthma sufferer, Spangler set out to find a way to keep dust from rising while he was sweeping floors. With a tin box, a fan, a pillow case, and a broom handle, he fashioned a crude, 40-pound device that pulled the dust away from him while he swept. The vacuum cleaner was born.

Spangler approached the Hoovers for financial backing to build and market the device. With a product endorsement from his wife, who had tried the device in the family home, William Hoover purchased the patent from Spangler in 1908 and incorporated The

Hoover Suction Sweeper Company. Spangler was retained as plant supervisor to help build manufacturing operations. In the first year, six employees built and sold nearly 350 "suction sweepers."

Electric cleaners were at first a sideline for the W.H. Hoover Company. A room in the leather goods factory was used, and the entire workforce numbered less than 20 people. The plant capacity was six to eight cleaners a day.

Hoover developed an ingenious marketing idea for his devices. He placed an ad in the local newspaper offering a free ten-day trial to anyone who submitted a written request. Rather than send the sweeper directly to those who answered the ad, Hoover sent the sweeper to a reputable store near the requester's home. He included a note, asking the store to deliver it to the person and, if a sale was made, told the store to keep the commission. This not only secured direct sales, it helped Hoover quickly establish a large network of dealers. On such ruses are brands built.

Hoover's fame soon spread beyond America. In 1911, he opened a Canadian assembly plant. Eight years later, he began a sales organization in England. Meanwhile the automobile was replacing the horse and buggy and the demand for harness and leather goods steadily declined. By 1919, it was decided to discontinue that part of the business and The Hoover Suction Sweeper Company (later shortened to the Hoover Company) centered all attention on the manufacture and sale of vacuum sweepers.

Hoover died on February 25, 1932. The Hoover brand continues to be one of the most recognized names in the floorcare industry. The company's main manufacturing facility is at the same site as William Hoover's first leather goods factory.

In recent years, *Fortune* magazine has featured its production line as one of the five American factories that rival the best in the world. The company has recently invested $47 million to expand its manufacturing facility in El Paso, Texas,

Maytag Corporation, Hoover's parent company, traces its origins to 1893 when F.L. Maytag began manufacturing farm implements in Newton, Iowa. In an effort to offset seasonal slumps in business, he introduced a wooden-tub washing machine in 1907.

The washing machines proved so popular that Maytag soon abandoned the farm implement business and devoted himself full-time to the washing machine business.

Today, in addition to Hoover, which was the company's fastest growing income stream in 1997, the company boasts a number of other leading brands including Maytag laundry and Jenn-Air. Overall, Maytag may rank third in total share and volume in the major appliance industry, but the company ranks much higher in the premium brand segments. Its premium brands are strongest at the more profitable, higher price points.

Best swept under the carpet

The Hoover brand had a rough time in the late 1980s and early 1990s. The economy dipped and the results of its parent company Maytag dipped with it. Hoover also provides a lesson. A misguided marketing promotion damaged the brand's credibility in the UK. What seemed at first a brilliant idea to boost sales – by offering free flights to Europe or the USA to any British customer who spent a minimum of £100 on Hoover products – turned into a corporate disaster. Marketing executives at Hoover miscalculated consumer tenacity, making the promotion vastly more expensive than anticipated.

The problem was brought to light not by the company, which must have known the tide of complaints was rising, but by media stories of angry customers who bought Hoover products, filled out their applications for tickets and then heard nothing from the company. The first mistake was then exacerbated by a series of subsequent blunders. These included a failure to act quickly enough to restore customer confidence and a public relations *faux pas* involving a comment from a Hoover manager that customers were foolish to expect something for nothing.

In April 1993, Maytag announced a net loss of $10.5 million in the first quarter, after taking a special charge of $30 million to cover the unexpected cost of the free flights promotion.

In other areas, too, the company has shown signs of brand fatigue. Poor performance at the start of the 1990s left analysts wondering whether the Maytag brand portfolio – including Hoover – was gathering dust.

In 1993, Maytag brought in a new CEO in the shape of Leonard A. Hadley. He restructured Maytag's balance sheet, reducing debt and interest expense by more than a third, and divested poorly performing businesses in order to reinvest in stronger core businesses.

As a result, he says, Maytag's business mix today is more clearly focused on what the company does best, where it competes best, and where it can grow profitably. It is targeted on the US and Canadian markets in North America and the Chinese market in Asia.

In particular, it has had to respond to the challenge from Dyson, the UK-based vacuum manufacture that is sweeping all before it. Hoover has introduced its own version of the Dyson cyclone system. It has patented its WindTunnel design.

Sucking up

The first Hoover cleaner weighed almost 40 pounds, because of the heavy motor required. In 1909, the development of the small high-speed fractional horsepower universal motor by Hamilton and Beach of Racine, Wisconsin, helped reduce the weight.

In that same year, Hoover established an engineering and design program of its own. Among its results was the development of the principle of carpet vibration for removal of dust. The original work on this principle was later developed to give Hoover cleaners an exclusive feature – the gentle beating or tapping of the carpet to loosen embedded dirt and grit by a spiral agitator bar.

This, in addition to the brushing action by revolving brushes, and strong suction, produced Hoover's famous "triple action," and inspired the well-known slogan: "It beats, as it sweeps, as it cleans."

In recent years, new competition has arrived in the shape of the Dyson. In response, Hoover has introduced its own version of the Dyson cyclone system – the Self Propelled WindTunnel upright. Whether such copycat innovations will be enough to protect its brand in future remains to be seen.

F ew business people create companies in their own image which then thrive after their departure. Most plummet after the final farewell from the great leader, unable or unwilling to carry on as before. Thomas Watson Senior (1874–1956), the man behind IBM, is one of the rare exceptions. Under Watson, IBM became the stuff of corporate and stock market legend, continuing to dominate long after Watson's death.

In his book, *A Business and Its Beliefs* – an extended IBM mission statement – Thomas Watson Jr later tellingly observed: "The beliefs that mold great organizations frequently grow out of the character, the experience and the convictions of a single person." In IBM's case that person was Thomas Watson Senior.

Watson created a brand that lasted. IBM – "Big Blue" – became the archetypal modern corporation and its managers the ultimate business stereotype – with their regulation sombre suits, white shirts, plain ties, zeal for selling and company song. Beneath this lay a belief in competing vigorously and providing quality service. Later, competitors complained that IBM's sheer size won it orders. This was only partly true. Its size masked a deeper commitment to managing customer accounts, providing service and building relationships. These elements were the cornerstones of the IBM brand and were established by the demanding perfectionist, Watson. In effect, Watson took branding beyond products. "He emphasized people and service – obsessively," noted Tom Peters in *Liberation Management*. "IBM was a service star in an era of malperforming machines." Service was the IBM brand.

The biggest meat slicer

IBM's origins lay in the semantically challenged Computing-Tabulating-Recording Company which Watson joined in 1914. Under Watson the company's revenues doubled from $4.2 million to $8.3 million by 1917. Initially making everything from butcher's scales to meat slicers, its activities gradually concentrated on tabulating machines that processed information mechanically on punched cards. Watson boldly renamed the company International Business Machines. This was, at the time, overstating the company's credentials though IBM Japan was established before World War II. (Brand lesson number one: sound big.)

IBM's development was helped by the 1937 Wages-Hours Act which required US companies to record hours worked and wages paid. The existing machines couldn't cope and Watson instigated work on a solution. In 1944 the Mark 1 was launched, followed by the Selective Sequence Electronic Calculator in 1947. By then IBM's revenues were $119 million and it was set to make the great leap forward to become the world's largest computer company and one of the world's most valuable bands.

While Thomas Watson Senior created IBM's service-centered brand and strong corporate culture, his son, Thomas Watson Junior (1914–1994) moved it from being an outstanding performer to world dominance. Watson Jr brought a vision of the future to the company, which his father had lacked. Yet, the strength of the original brand remained intact.

While some regard Watson Jr simply as the son who inherited control of a corporate juggernaut and did little to put his own stamp on its destination, others see him as the man who brought IBM into the technological era and who mapped out how values and culture could shape an entire organization. In 1987 Watson was hailed by *Fortune* as "the most successful capitalist in history." (This, of course, was the kiss of death.)

Whichever interpretation is correct, Watson had a significant role in the shaping of the modern IBM – a company whose trials and tribulations continue to fill the media. Watson Jr was always in the shadow of his father – "The secret I learned early on from my father was to run scared and never think I had made it," he said – but under him IBM was propelled to the forefront of the technological and corporate revolution of the 1960s and 1970s. Most notably, the 1962 decision to develop the System/360 family of computers cost the company $5 billion – more than the development costs of the atomic bomb. The result was the first mainframe computer, even though IBM's market research suggested it would only sell two units worldwide. System/360 formed the basis of the company's success in the 1970s and 1980s.

Watson's real claim to managerial fame does not, however, lie in the company's technological achievements. Indeed, these were something he himself sometimes questioned. In 1965, Watson despaired at IBM's weak response to Seymour Cray's development of the CDC 6600. "Contrasting this modest effort with 34 people including the janitor with our vast development activities, I fail to understand why we have lost our industry leadership position by letting someone else offer the world's most powerful computer," said Watson. How could a minnow out-innovate a giant? Cray had a quick riposte: "It seems Mr Watson has answered his own question."

In terms of management thinking, what IBM stood for was more important than what it made. Under Watson, the corporate culture, the company's values and the company brand became all-important. They were the glue that kept a sprawling international operation under control.

The three basic beliefs on which IBM was built were: give full consideration to the individual employee; spend a lot of time making customers happy; and go the last mile to do things right. These had been established under Watson Sr. But, while Watson Sr was content to drum the message home, his son took it a step further.

Watson Jr. codified and clarified what IBM stood for. Beliefs, he said, never change. Change everything else, but never the basic truths on which the company is based – "If an organization is to meet the challenges of a changing world, it must be prepared to change everything about itself except beliefs as it moves through corporate life…The only sacred cow in an organization should be its basic philosophy of doing business."

Whether IBM collapsed because it failed to change or adapt its beliefs to new times is difficult to determine. Watson saw it coming.

"I'm worried that IBM could become a big, inflexible organization which won't be able to change when the computer business goes through its next shift," Watson told Chris Argyris of Harvard in the 1950s when Argyris did some work for the company. Watson saw the future but couldn't mobilize the corporate culture he did so much to clarify in structures or practices which enabled IBM to pick up the baton.

The fall and rise of Big Blue

If a product or service has become indistinguishable from its rivals, it has become a commodity. A commodity – like coffee, oil or aluminium – sells chiefly on price. This happened to personal computers (PCs) in the 1980s. Previously, consumers had been wooed by the brand difference offered by IBM. This came in the form of security, confidence and quality. At one point, IBM earned 70 percent of the worldwide computer industry's profits.

When companies and consumers realized that PCs were indistinguishable there was no need to pay extra for IBM's brand. (IBM's gross profit margins fell from 55 percent in 1990 to 38 percent in 1993.) Reassurance went out of the window. As a result, cheap clones knocked IBM from its lofty perch.

The IBM brand was ranked third in the world in 1993 and by the 1994 league tables was rated as having a negative value. "For 20 years IBM was in charge of the transformation agenda in the computer industry. Then the industry became driven by the vision and strategy of other companies. IBM's problems are not about implementation but foresight," says contemporary strategy guru Gary Hamel.

The fall of IBM provides an object lesson in what not to do when handling powerful brands. Wharton's George S Day has argued that central to IBM's fall was that it became "self-centered."[1] IBM became distant from its customers. Customer information was poorly captured and distributed. Senior managers became ever more distant from what was happening in the market place. (One critic compared IBM to a music publishing company run by deaf people.)

In addition, its undoubted centers of excellence existed in isolation. IBM continued to sustain superb standards, but lacked any means of delivering such excellence on a broader scale. IBM also began to concentrate on cost reduction to achieve short-term financial results rather than on long-term development.

Day also contends that IBM fell into what he calls "the customer compulsion trap" – though this time in the early 1990s. In effect, IBM sought to redress the balance by listening to each and every one of its customers. The result was confusion and disillusionment. At the beginning of the 1990s, IBM stared into the corporate precipice. Big Blue, the symbol of American corporate might recorded massive losses and seemed too out of touch with the marketplace to make a comeback.

Then it recruited former McKinsey consultant and turnaround master Lou Gerstner. When he became CEO in 1993, Gerstner decided not to split IBM – something which previous CEO, John Akers had prepared for. The company's revitalization owes a great deal to this decision. Gerstner also reflected that IBM had been through "an economic shock the equivalent of an earthquake."

Under Gerstner, IBM has made a surprisingly strong recovery. It has got back in touch. Take its role in Internet development. In 1993, long-serving IBM-er John Patrick was arguing that everyone at the company should have their own e-mail address and that the company needed a web site. "Connect with other people. If you become externally focused, you can change the whole company," said Patrick. What is interesting is that Patrick's call to arms was basically a return to the company's first principles – get in touch with customers and communicate internally. The only difference was that Patrick was championing the latest technology to do so.[2]

As proof that IBM's culture has changed, forces were mobilized in a way the slow moving monolith of the past never even contemplated. In 1995 only two of the company's 220,000 employees were working on Java. By 1997, 2400 scientists and engineers throughout the world were doing so. Indeed, such is the cultural change that parts of IBM more resemble Microsoft. There is talk of breaking rules, using small eccentric groups to tackle problems from different angles, to bring fresh thinking.

Lou Gerstner stalks in the background, pulling the strings, exerting pressure when needed. In fact, his behavior appears to be a textbook example of modern leadership – empowering and coaching rather than controlling. At the same time, his feet appear firmly planted in commercial reality. Says Gerstner: "My view is you perpetuate success by continuing to run scared, not by looking back at what made you great, but looking forward at what is going to make you ungreat, so that you are constantly focusing on the challenges that keep you humble, hungry and nimble."[3]

Typically, when Gerstner was shown the Internet for the first time his reaction was "This is great, this is a new channel for business. How do we make it real for customers? How do we make money on it?" The order of these priorities – customers and then profit – is perhaps the vital lesson from IBM's renaissance and the rise, fall and rise of the IBM brand.

Notes

1   Day, George S., "What does it mean to be market-driven?" *Business Strategy Review*, Spring 1998.

2   Ransdell, Eric, "IBM's grassroots revival," *Fast Company*, October–November 1997.

3   Kehoe, Louise, "Big Blue-eyed boy makes good," *Financial Times*, April 22, 1995.

Ikea is one of the great retail brands of our times. The Swedish furniture company has endeared itself to younger, price-conscious home makers around the world. To them, Ikea – with its DIY assembly from flat-packs – represents stylish design at affordable prices. To the loyal customers who fill its stores Ikea is self-assemble chic.

Rising from its humble origins in Small-land, a rural area of Sweden, Ikea has grown from a tiny mail order business to a $5.8 billion furniture giant. The brand is driven by the philosophies of its founder Ingvar Kamprad – from whose initials the company partly derives its name.

Ikea now operates more than 140 stores in 28 countries and employs about 35,000 people. The "Ikea way" enshrines a set of values that have ensured an almost unrivalled communion with its customers. A simple white lacquered bookshelf called Billy, has been selling well for 20 years. Such lucrative simplicity is testimony to the fact that Ikea knows the minds of its customers.

In recent years, however, the darling of the 20- and 30-somethings has received a rough ride from the media. Revelations about Kamprad's past – his Nazi sympathies in his youth and his drinking habits – did little to enhance the brand's wholesome appeal. In these more forgiving days, however, even billionaire entrepreneurs are allowed a few skeletons in the closet.

In Britain, the company was also criticized for its slowness in reacting to customer complaints and manufacturing faults. Such problems prove, perhaps, that you really can't please all the people all the time. But they also highlight the difficulty of operating what is now a large international business using a "small company management philosophy."

Swedish customers, who know the company's heritage, might be inclined to give Ikea the benefit of the doubt when problems arise.

But many of the people visiting its stores overseas know nothing of its origins.

From humble beginnings

The Ikea story began in the 1930s. The company grew out of the vision of Ingvar Kamprad. That vision – created years before Anita Roddick's Body Shop and other new age brands – remains the guiding principle for the business today.

It is summed up in a mission statement: "To contribute to a better everyday working life for the majority of people, by offering a wide range of home furnishing items of good design and function, at prices so low that the majority of people can afford to buy them."

Born in the barren country of Small-land in Sweden, Kamprad grew up during the Great Depression. He took the qualities of resourcefulness he saw around him to heart. The thrifty, hard working ideals of his Swedish homeland were applied to the retail business. Starting with matches he moved onto furniture and ended up with one of the largest furniture retailers in the world. Now in his 70s, he refers to the values he instilled in Ikea as the "testament of a furniture dealer."

It's a home-spun philosophy which combines the virtues of simplicity and making do, with a commitment to equality and innovation. It's an approach in step with today's times. The company was one of the first to use recycled materials in furniture, for example, more out of a desire to keep costs down than to be seen as green.

Building on its early experience in Sweden – when a visit to an Ikea store could involve a day's travel – the company has developed a distinctively integrated approach to retailing which aims to make shopping an enjoyable experience rather than a chore.

Cynics may question whether its folksy, for the people, philosophy can truly survive the transition to a big business, but the Ikea employees are genuinely committed to it. According to one senior Ikea executive at the company's headquarters in the Swedish town of Almhult: "The only way of keeping the customer long-term in our vision is that he has a benefit from coming to Ikea. The product and price quality that we offer must be the best. We even say that we must have better prices than our competitors as one of our operating principles. That is basic to our long-term success.

"From there we say how can we make a visit to Ikea a day out? Ikea should be a day out. That started in the first store here in Almhult. In the old days to come to our store they had to leave early in the morning. The journey would usually take a couple of hours and many of our customers had small children." Hence the family restaurants and crèche facilities that have become a feature of Ikea stores (on weekends and holidays, the company even employs clowns and magicians to entertain the kids).

The logic is pragmatic. "We believe that the prices in our restaurants should be very good so that customers with young families can afford to eat there and do not have to bring sandwiches. They shouldn't have to leave Ikea just because they are hungry."

The same sort of egalitarian principles apply to the management culture. Ikea permits no status symbols and refers to all employees as co-workers. The philosophy is reinforced by the example of Anders Moburg, the company's current President, who was hand-picked by Kamprad. When travelling on business, for example, Moburg is famous for flying economy class, and refuses to take taxis when public transport is available. True to its small company roots, too, Ikea carries out relatively little customer research into new products, relying instead on a feel for the market.

As Jan Kjellmam, head of its Swedish division where the international design team is located, explained: "We don't ask so many questions before we start up things. We launched the "Swedish Cottage" range without any market research, but the customer liked it very much."

In recent years, Ikea has also succeeded where many European retailers have failed, successfully taking its formula to North America. The experience, however, was not without lessons. Puzzled at first by poor sales of beds and other lines, it quickly learned that although Americans liked the simplicity of its designs they wanted furniture to match their larger homes. The answer? Bigger furniture.

In 1997, Ikea introduced a new line of children's furniture and toys, and the company continues to invest in new stores. There are plans to expand extensively in Eastern Europe. Ten stores are planned in Poland by 2000 as well as opening in Bulgaria, Romania, and Russia. Next stop Asia.

With a $10 million investment to date in Shanghai, China, and $130 million on retail and distribution networks in Taiwan and Hong Kong the most serious cloud on the horizon is the issue of succession. In his 70s Kamprad has relinquished formal control to Moberg but remains an active presence. Whether the company can continue its success without the idiosyncratic touch of its founder remains to be seen.

But the omens are good. Despite prices up to 30 percent cheaper than rivals, in 1997 sales were up 21 percent for the year. Somehow Ikea continues to squeeze increasing returns from its retail units; it has been estimated that sales per square meter are twice the industry's average. Analysts say Ikea's stores generate about $43 million a year in revenues. With low debt and strong cash flow, Ikea is able to finance expansion from its own pockets.

Ikea remains privately owned. Its capital has been estimated at £2.69 billion. "Ikea itself is a money machine," concluded Stellan Bjork, author of a book about the company. Few could disagree.

I n 1968, Gordon Moore and Robert Noyce left Fairchild Semiconductor to establish their own company, Intel. The rest is a whirlwind of technological history and huge commercial success. They were joined in their adventure by employee #4, Andy Grove and, along the way, Gordon Moore came up with the most-quoted law of Silicon Valley – Moore's Law that the number of electronic elements that can be written on the same size chip will double every 18 months.

The technological leaps forward started early in Intel's life. In 1971 it introduced the world's first microprocessor, the 4004. Intel also invented the high speed-memory (D-RAM) used in every kind of computer system. Such was its success that Intel had 10,000 employees by 1977. In the 1980s, Intel shrewdly refused to give other manufacturers a licence to make its most powerful chips. So, it made them all. In 1981, an IBM PC based on the Intel microprocessor was launched. This helped sales reach $1 billion for the first time in 1984. A blip in 1986 saw Intel record a loss for the first time, but it speedily returned to profit in 1987 and in 1990 racked up its first $1 billion quarter, quickly followed, three years later, by its first $2 billion quarter.

The basic premise of Intel's success is simply put by Andy Grove: "Business is about communications, sharing data and instantaneous decision making. If you have on your desk a device that enables you to communicate and share data with your colleagues around the world, you will have a strategic advantage."[1]

Branding inside

For most of this time, Intel was unbranded and unknown. Only Silicon Valley insiders and computer enthusiasts are really interested in where the chips come from. Even though it already held over 80 percent of the PC-chip market, Intel decided that it wanted to become a known brand as well as extremely successful. Intel wanted everyone to be aware what was inside computers doing the real work. The result was its Intel Inside campaign, which was hugely expensive and successful. People are now aware that Intel makes chips. From nowhere, Intel became a top-ranking brand. By 1993 Intel was voted the world's third most valuable brand by *Financial World* magazine. Valued at $17.8 billion (compared to the worth of its nearest competitor at $4.1 billion), Intel only lagged behind Marlboro and Coca Cola. Quite an achievement.

Intel followed up its initial campaign with one for its Pentium chip. The logic behind this was that the Pentium was the newest and most powerful PC-chip on the market. The Pentium was Intel's successor to the highly successful 266, 386 and 486 chips.

After its launch at the beginning of 1994, Intel anticipated sales of the Pentium would reach in excess of 10 million units by 1996. The campaign encouraged people to switch from 486 machines to Pentium PCs. All very laudable but, as Intel made the 486 chips, the company was waging a campaign against itself. The campaign worked – it increased awareness of the Pentium … and also succeeded in annoying companies, such as Compaq, which were still putting their efforts into selling 486s. Compaq's marketing needed to find ways round the suggestion from the chip maker that the 486 was basically obsolete.

Of course, having revealed to the world that it makes the chips, Intel's troubles begin if the chips go wrong. It may be three million transistors on a minute bit of silicon, but we expect it to be perfect and, thanks to Intel's marketing, if there is a fault in the chip we now know who to blame. Forget Dell or IBM, call Intel.

"With Intel Inside you know you've got … unparalleled quality," read an Intel advertisement. The "unparalleled quality" boast appeared a little excessive late in 1994 when Thomas Nicely, a mathematics professor at Lynchburg College, Virginia, achieved international renown. Professor Nicely found that his three Pentium computers were making mistakes and then, in an effort to get to the bottom of the mystery, shared his discovery on the Internet. Thanks to the miracles of modern technology, a minor mathematical problem became an international incident. And, thanks to Intel's advertising, people knew where the fault lay.

In December 1994, IBM announced that it was halting shipments of the affected PCs and Intel was forced to adopt a vigorous damage limitation exercise. Intel's first reaction was that IBM's tests were "contrived."

The fault was small – Intel calculated it would afflict the average user only once every 27,000 years; IBM countered that some customers could encounter the fault every month. "For a customer with 500 Pentium-based PCs, this could result in as many as 20 mistakes a day," said IBM. Coincidentally, IBM was also developing machines with its own chip – "After years watching Intel build its brand at IBM's expense, Big Blue must have found this as emotionally satisfying as a long-suffering sugar daddy cancelling an errant mistress's credit card," observed *The Economist*.[2]

Whatever the nature and regularity of the flaw, Intel clearly had set itself up. Ironically, the problem with the Pentium was far less significant than flaws found in previous chips – the only difference was that Intel had marketed the brand too successfully. Not only had five million Pentiums been manufactured, but the Pentium was backed by an $80 million marketing campaign to encourage the market to make the switch from the old (the 486) to the new (the Pentium). This came on top of the estimated $70 million spent on the Intel Inside campaigns.

Intel's problems were largely of its own making. It created the brand and has to live with the consequences. Also, it is clearly a victim of its own success. The bigger the name, the bigger the brand, the keener competitors, onlookers, commentators and journalists are to topple it from its pedestal.

The media attention over the Pentium is one of the few false moves in the company's entire history. Andy Grove's initial pronouncements seemed to suggest that the controversy was caused by ignorance and media hype – "We are quite clearly anxious to have this event behind us, but given that this has become a major event in the mass media, involving people who are not accustomed to dealing with sophisticated mathematical terms like random divides, operands and floating points, quite frankly we don't know what to do," said Grove.[3]

Initially Intel offered to replace chips for customers who could prove that their machines were needed for accurate complex computations. It was only later in December that it offered to replace processors free of charge. "Our previous policy was to talk with users to determine whether their needs required replacement of the processor. There was a resentment to our approach – it appeared that we at Intel were arrogant, we were telling customers what was good for them. Maybe we have been thick-headed....but we finally figured it out," observed Andy Grove.[4] On 22 December 1994 Intel took a full-page advertisement in the *Financial Times* to apologize – "No microprocessor is ever perfect," it said "What Intel continues to believe is that an extremely minor technical problem has taken on a life of its own. Although Intel firmly stands behind the quality of the current version of the Pentium processor, we recognize that many users have concerns. We want to resolve these concerns."

As Moore's Law predicts, such distractions quickly become history. Technology and Intel move on. The focus of Intel's marketing has moved from selling product features in the early 1970s to direct partnership with the final customers of the company's microprocessors. It has moved on with remorseless speed and a rare clarity of purpose and thinking.

Chips and gravy

- 1968: Intel founded with the aim of making semiconductor memory practical.
- 1971: 4004 microcomputer introduced – managed 60,000 operations in one second. Followed by the 8008.
- Mid-1970s: "In the mid-1970s, someone came to me with an idea for what was basically the PC," Gordon Moore recalls. "I personally didn't see anything useful in it, so we never gave it another thought."
- 1981: Intel's range included the 8086 and 8088 processors. IBM selected the 8088 as the basis of the first PC.
- 1982: 286 chip.
- 1985: 386 processor – over 5 million instructions per second.
- 1989: 486 processor – 50 times faster than the 4004.
- 1993: Pentium – 1,500 times faster than the 4004.
- 1995: Pentium Pro.
- 1997: MMX technology introduced to enhance multimedia performance; Pentium II.
- 1998: Celeron processor.

Notes

1   Cane, Alan, "Chips with everything," *Financial Times*, November 15, 1993.
2   "Intel's chip of worms?" *The Economist*, December 17, 1994.
3   Kehoe, Louise, "Article of faith challenged," *Financial Times*, December 14, 1994.
4   Kehoe, Louise, "Intel offers to replace Pentium microchips," *Financial Times*, December 21, 1994.

T he Kellogg logo is invited to breakfast in more homes around the world than any other brand. The company has dominated the breakfast cereals market for decades, and owns 12 of the top cereal brands – including Corn Flakes, Rice Krispies and Froot Loops.

William Keith Kellogg, who started mass-producing corn flakes in 1906, insisted on high quality standards, and took great care over every detail of production. Counterfeit products were a problem even then. To ensure that customers would not buy inferior imitations he had his signature printed on every packet. Leading brands have been using similar strategies ever since.

At its zenith in 1988, the company enjoyed more than 40 percent of the US ready-to-eat market. Since then, however, lower priced store brands have begun to take a bigger bite out of the $8 billion American cereal market.

In 1997, Kellogg, the industry leader, was still deriving 80 percent of its worldwide sales from cereal. In the U.S., however, the cereal market is barely growing, with consumers switching to bagels and other breakfast products they can eat on the move.

Despite its huge market presence and instant consumer recognition, in the next few years Kellogg faces some tough decisions. It offers a fascinating snap shot of one of the world's great brand companies at a critical moment in its history.

The first bowl

In 1876, Dr John Harvey Kellogg was appointed chief physician of the Western Health Reform Institute in Battle Creek, Michigan. The organization was inspired by the wife of a church minister who had the idea that a diet based on grains, nuts and vegetable foods had an uplifting and purifying effect on the soul. Dr Kellogg became interested in a product that would be good for the body, developing a easy-to-digest breakfast to replace the stodgy traditional fare.

With his brother William Keith Kellogg, he invented a wafer-thin malt-flavored toasted flake, which proved popular with patients. So popular in fact that he was inundated with orders from former patients, asking for the product to be posted to them. It was the beginning of the breakfast table phenomenon known as corn flakes.

In 1906, William Keith established the Battle Creek Toasted Corn Flake Company in a wooden shed. The building burned down within a year, and he was forced to build new, bigger, premises.

Kellogg was an early convert to advertising, and used the new medium to good effect. Sales grew. By 1909, production had leapt from an initial 33 cases per day to over a million. The 1911 advertising budget was $1 million. In 1912, Kellogg installed the world's largest sign in Times Square, New York. The K in the word Kellogg's was 60 feet high.

In the 1940s, Kellogg's recognized the growing marketing power of health, and began adding nutrients and vitamins to its grains. In 1955, the company introduced Special K, a cereal with added protein.

Over the years, more products were added to the range, but Corn Flakes remained the biggest seller. By 1986, Kellogg had 22 plants operating in 17 countries and annual sales in excess of $6 billion.

In recent years, however, Kellogg's has drawn criticism for the way it has managed its brands. A headline in *Fortune* in August 1997, asked: "Where did the Snap, Crackle & Pop go?" The article went on to claim that: "Kellogg's unimaginative management team is slowly spoiling some of the world's top brands."[1]

What prompted the bad press in part was a lack of urgency or fresh ideas emanating from the Kellogg's headquarters in Battle Creek. From its seemingly unassailable position in 1988 when the company's brands accounted for 40.5 percent of the US cereals market, by 1997 the figure had fallen to 33.2 percent.

Like its nearest rivals General Mills (Wheaties, Cheerios), Philip Morris' Post (Grape Nuts, Shredded Wheat) and Quaker Oats,

Kellogg's was under attack from own label store brands which had doubled their market share to 10 percent over the same period. The problem for Kellogg and its rivals was that they were caught in a zero-sum game; the total US market is barely growing.

Kellogg's price raising strategy – sometimes hiking prices twice in the same year – had taken its toll, even though it was offset with coupon promotions. The turning point came when a packet of Kellogg's Apple Jacks broke through the $5 barrier. Consumers, tired of endlessly clipping coupons, began buying own label cereals and switching to bagels.

Kellogg's CEO Arnold Langbo told Wall Street analysts, impatient to see some action by the company, that 1997 would be the year the company got serious about growth. But early signs were disappointing. What Langbo did do was begin to restructure the Kellogg's leviathan, closing factories and cutting jobs.

The dilemma facing Kellogg's is one that all great brands have to face at some time. Premium price brands are seductive. It is easy to think that if you own the market, leave well alone. Why fix something that isn't broken? It can be dangerous to meddle with a winning formula (as Coke discovered). But the flip-side is that without innovation it is hard to justify price increases, and the brand begins to die.

As one leading consultant noted: "Kellogg's is a great company with extraordinary potential, wrestling with issues that other companies, such as Gillette, Procter & Gamble, and Anheuser-Busch have faced – how to maximize famous brands and retain their premium images without overpricing them. Whether Kellogg's will emerge from this struggle stronger or weaker is a question."

For now, that question remains unanswered. At the beginning of 1999, the company announced that Arnold Langbo was stepping down, to be replaced as CEO by Carlos Gutierrez. Langbo will remain as chairman until 2000. On the announcement of his appointment Gutierrez observed: "I am convinced that the key to growth for our company and the category is investment in product innovation, in franchise-building marketing and in the accelerated expansion of our convenience foods business."

Note

1   Grant, Linda, "Where did the Snap, Crackle & Pop go?" *Fortune*, August 4, 1997.

odern advertising can be said to begin," one writer noted, "with the slogan 'You press the button; we do the rest.'" It was the birth of snapshot photography as millions of amateur picture-takers know it today.

The man who wrote that slogan was George Eastman, pioneer of early photographic film and founder of Eastman Kodak. In 1888, he put the first simple camera into the hands of a world of consumers and made what had been a complicated process easy to use and accessible to all. Eastman was the father of a particular type of branding: "Trust what's in the box" branding.

Today, the original Kodak proposition is implicit in the positioning of countless branded gadgets that we now take for granted. With it's suggestion that consumers need provide just their imagination to complement its technology, Microsoft's "Where do you want to go today?", for instance, is a modern echo of that first Kodak promise, as is "Intel Inside." Both draw on Eastman's early inspiration that consumers should trust the brand to take care of the technology side, leaving them free to personalize the product to their own lives.

Like no other slogan, Eastman's captured a turning point in the history of consumerism. Previously, consumers had understood – even if only at a rudimentary level – how the products they bought worked. But in the late 19th and early 20th century, an explosion of new inventions – which included the telephone, the electric light bulb and film processing – meant that changed forever.

Eastman was the product of a remarkable moment in history. He was one of a special breed of pioneers at the end of the nineteenth century who redefined the frontiers of consumerism by applying the new science and technology bubbling up from a thousand creative springs. Eastman himself dropped out of high school at the age of 13, and in the tradition of US entrepreneurs used his vision in the application of science to a mass market product.

The name "Kodak" was first registered as a trademark in 1888. Its origins have been the centre of speculation ever since, but Eastman appears to have invented it out of thin air.

"I devised the name myself," he told his biographer. "The letter 'K' had been a favourite with me – it seems a strong incisive sort of letter. It became a question of trying out a great number of combinations of letters that made words starting and ending with K. The word Kodak is the result."

The name and the brand's distinctive yellow and black colors, also selected by Eastman, are one of the company's most valuable assets today. They owe their origins to Eastman's unbounded belief in the power of advertising.

Early Kodak products were advertised in leading newspapers and periodicals of the day – with ads written by Eastman himself. In 1897, the word Kodak sparkled from an electric sign on London's Trafalgar Square – one of the first signs of its kind to be used in advertising. Later, space was taken at world events such as the World Fairs and the Olympic Games.

In time, the "Kodak Girl" was born. Brilliantly conceived, she combined sex appeal with an ever-changing wardrobe that kept the Kodak brand image fresh. Her image smiled at photographers from advertisements and the style of her clothes and camera changed every year.

Innovation has always been integral to the brand. Over the years, Kodak has led the way with a plethora of new products and processes that made photography simpler, more useful and more enjoyable. This has earned Kodak a special place in America's memories. It was fitting that when John Glenn became the first American astronaut to orbit the earth, Kodak film recorded his reactions to travelling through space.

In recent years, the company has drawn on its emotional relationship with the many consumers whose memories are recorded on its film. Millions of Americans shared their most treasured moments with Kodak. To enhance the company's mission of encouraging people to capture and share memories, it launched its "Take Pictures Further" campaign. The slogan featured a series of TV commercials designed to broaden the appeal of the Kodak brand to a wider cross section of consumers and business decision makers.

In 1996, US consumers once again picked the Kodak brand as the most widely recognized and respected brand in the world, in the EquiTrend brand equity survey conducted by Total Research Corporation. But the past decade has been a bumpy ride. The Kodak brand was not enough to protect it from the ravages of competition.

In the late 1980s and early 1990s, hapless Kodak managers watched competitors like Fuji Photo Film and others devour 30 percent of the company's market for film sales. By 1993, one of America's best known names and one of the world's most famous brands looked in danger of extinction.

As *Fortune* noted: "The company had gone through five separate restructurings, 40,000 jobs had disappeared, and $10 billion spent to diversify had pushed debt up to 69 percent of total capital. But all that produced little, and the stock faltered."[1]

In 1993 exasperated directors finally fired former chairman Kay Whitmore and, led by Coca-Cola Chairman Roberto Goizueta, persuaded ex-Motorola boss George Fisher to step into the hot seat and try to reverse Kodak's fortunes.

As CEO of Motorola, Fisher had steered the cellular phone business from infancy to no. 1. But fixing Kodak was never going to be easy. One Wall Street analyst observed that turning the company around would require "one of the greatest feats in business annals."

What made analysts all the more skeptical was that Fisher was no downsizer. At a time when other US companies were engaged in vicious cost cutting, Kodak sought to repair itself by more humanitarian means. Those who knew Fisher's style, were not surprised. University of Michigan business professor C.K. Prahalad predicted at the time: "George has no interest in implementing a cut, slash, and burn operation. He is going to take his time to think, reconfigure, readapt, reposition, and grow the company."

Prahalad's view was prescient. Fisher set about a methodical rebuilding of confidence among Kodak's shell-shocked ranks while divesting a rag bag of diversified interests and refocusing the company on its core business of photography.

The initial results were encouraging. After 1993 debt fell to 19 percent of capital, and analysts anticipated that Kodak would earn about $1.5 billion on sales of $16 billion in 1996. But a combination of a bruising price war with Fuji Film and a high dollar took its toll. This was compounded by other problems – notably in R&D, where Kodak invested $100 million in an advanced–photo-system camera and film, only to find that it could not fill store shelves and could not process the film at enough locations.

By 1997 Kodak had begun to falter – falling back from 20 percent growth to just seven, and losing three to four points of market share to Fuji. The company's famously paternalistic approach to employees became unsustainable. Fisher was forced to cut costs. He cut 200 management jobs – including the heads of the company's three most critical businesses, consumer imaging; Kodak professional; and digital and applied imaging – and 16,600 other employees.

R&D was re-vamped. In 1998, the company sank another $100 million into the advanced-photo-system, but took a more focused approach advocated by its new marketing head Daniel Palumbo, who joined from Procter & Gamble.

Research showed that one-third of all camera buyers wanted cameras for under $50. The Kodak models had been priced higher. But with the re-launch of the advanced-photo-system – a cross between a digital and analog camera – the prices came down. The new product range did well, accounting for 20 percent of all Kodak sales during the 1997 Christmas season.

With analysis revealing that 80 percent of all Kodak sales come from just 20 percent of the product line, the company also eliminated 27 percent of all sales items, revamped its packaging and boosted the advertising spend.

The new in-store brand proposition centered on three offerings of Kodak film:

- Max, with two speeds of film to satisfy most needs. It also features the company's one-time-use camera called Max. "It's our version of "Intel Inside," Palumbo said at the brand re-launch.
- Second, there is Kodak Gold – aimed at price sensitive consumers who have drifted to Fuji in recent years.
- Third, for specialists and enthusiasts there is the Select Group – Advantix, Royal Gold, Elite and Kodachrome.

Today, Kodak is competing not just with arch rival Fuji but with hungry Silicon Valley predators in search of a share of the emerging digital-photo market. The challenge facing the company is to transform itself into a high-performing organization, capable of holding its own with the likes of Canon and Microsoft.

As marketing expert and Harvard Business School professor John Kotter has observed: "This is a howlingly, horrifically difficult challenge. For a century Kodak had too much success and too much market share. It was as bad as IBM at its worst."

The next few years will tell whether one of America's best known companies re-invents itself for the digital age, or limps quietly into the sunset. Either way, the Kodak brand is likely to survive in one form or another – it is too valuable to be allowed to die.

CEO George Fisher observed of the company's remarkable founder: "Like Alexander Graham Bell, Eastman tinkered his way to a universally welcome invention. Like Henry Ford, he put his name on his company. Like Thomas Eddison, he shaped his products to world markets hungry for their startling benefits."

Snapshots of a brand

- 1879: Eastman invented an emulsion-coating machine that enabled him to mass-produce photographic dry plates.
- 1880: Eastman began commercial production of dry plates in a rented loft in Rochester, N.Y.

- 1881: Eastman and Henry A. Strong formed a partnership known as the Eastman Dry Plate Company; Eastman quit his job as a bank clerk to devote his full time to the business.
- 1883: Moved to what is now 343 State Street, Rochester, NY, the company's worldwide headquarters.
- 1885: Eastman American Film was introduced – the first transparent photographic "film" as we know it today.
- 1888: The name "Kodak" was born and the Kodak Camera was placed on the market, with the slogan, "You push the button – we do the rest."
- 1889: The first commercial transparent roll film.
- 1891: First daylight-loading camera.
- 1892: The company became Eastman Kodak Company of New York.
- 1895: The Pocket Kodak Camera.
- 1898: The Folding Pocket Kodak Camera.
- 1900: The first of the famous Brownie Cameras introduced.
- 1917: Kodak developed aerial cameras and trained aerial photographers for the US Signal Corps during World War I.
- 1932: George Eastman died, leaving his entire residual estate to the University of Rochester.
- 1950: Unveiled the first in its long-running series of Kodak Colorama Display transparencies – 18 feet high and 60 feet wide – overlooking the main terminal floor of Grand Central Station in New York City.
- 1951: Low-priced Brownie 8 mm Movie Camera introduced.
- 1955: Began selling color films without the cost of processing included, as the result of a consent decree signed in 1954.
- 1961: Introduced the first in its very successful line of Kodak Carousel Projectors.
- 1962: Sales exceeded $1 billion for the first time.
- 1963: Kodak Instamatic Cameras introduced.
- 1972: Sales passed $4 billion.
- 1982: Launched "disc photography."

- 1993: Kodak CEO Kay Whitemore replaced by George M.C. Fisher.
- 1995: Kodak Digital Science brand mark unveiled.
- 1996: Introduced the Advantix brand.
- 1997: Kodak picture network announced.

Notes

1   Grant, Linda, "Can Fisher focus Kodak?" *Fortune*, January 13, 1996.

Lego

Few brands are as aptly named as Lego. Ole Kirk Christiansen, the company's founder, built the name by putting the Danish words play well (*leg* and *godt*) together. From the early wooden toys, the company moved to the familiar brightly colored nobuled bricks. Generations of children have grown up constructing their fantasy worlds and inventions out of Lego.

More than just a toy, Lego was re-launched in the 1950s as a "system of play." Anyone who has ever watched children playing with Lego will know just how absorbing an activity it can be. (In Latin, Lego actually means "I am reading" or "I am joining together.")

The Lego principle – interchangeable components that can be endlessly reconfigured by the imaginative mind of a child – has been copied many times by many toy manufacturers. But the appeal of the original remains unrivalled. The power of Lego is that it is easy to use – requiring no special tools or parental help – and endlessly adaptable. It is, quite simply, a different toy for every child each day.

Lego also appeals to a wide range of ages. Toddlers start out with the extra large Duplo bricks before moving onto the standard size Lego. Sets come in all sizes and are priced to fit all pockets. Over time, a child can collect more and more pieces to take on ever larger construction projects. Some children get hooked and carry on the passion as adults.

From a parental point of view, Lego is hard to beat. It is clean, safe and non-violent. It also has educational properties as children learn to manipulate the bricks and to realize their imagination. Many a parent has spent hours creating some complicated Lego grand design only to find the ungrateful offspring gleefully disassembling it a few minutes later.

Building the Lego empire

In the depression of the 1930s, Ole Kirk Christiansen was made redundant from his job in Denmark. A carpenter by trade, he lived in the tiny village of Billund on the moors of Jutland. With time on his hands, he had an idea that he could fashion quality toys that would appeal to a child's imagination and creative instincts. His toys would be robust and capable of withstanding rough treatment.

He made yo-yos, elephants on wheels, miniature baby carriages, model automobiles and a host of other designs. A pull-along duck was the best-seller of its day. In time, his wooden toys became popular and he began employing other craftsmen.

By the late 1940s, Lego employed some 50 staff and had grown to become the largest company in the area. Christiansen's son Gotfred, who had worked with his father from the age of 14, traveled to England. On his journey he discussed a new concept for a toy with a toy dealer who was looking for a radically different sort of product – something with purpose and continuity.

The idea appealed to Gotfred. He felt the answer lay with bricks – which could be used to literally build another world. It would be possible to put these bricks together and take them apart.

In 1955, after a great deal of trial and experimentation, the now famous Lego brick was launched in Denmark. Unlike the company's previous products, the new product was a complete "system of play." It was aimed at boys and girls of all ages. It was simple, endlessly versatile, and immensely satisfying to play with.

By the time Ole Kirk Christiansen died in 1958, and Gotfred took over, the new Lego play system was already a success. The business had a turnover in excess of $1.5 million. It moved into an entirely new sphere in 1968 when the company created the first Legoland. A ten acre site near the Lego factory was landscaped into a children's paradise, and included model villages, cafes, dolls museums and other attractions. Today, the original Legoland attracts more than a million visitors a year.

In 1968, Lego added wheels to its play system, opening up new avenues – and highways – to the children who played with it. Lego play figures followed, and in 1977 Lego Technical Sets were introduced so that working models could be made.

In 1993, Lego launched children's clothes as a brand extension. Lego Kids' Mix & Match Wear grew out of a licencing arrangement with between the company and the Danish clothing manufacturer Kabooki, and are sold at outlets throughout Scandinavia and Holland.

Today, the company exports to more than 100 countries all over the world. Some 97 percent of the production at the company's factory in Billund is for export.

Young at heart

Few businesses are as fashion driven as the toy industry. In recent years, the onslaught of television advertising at Christmas means that children are acutely aware of what's hot and what's old news. Amid a maelstrom of manipulative marketing, Lego has skillfully kept its toys contemporary through constant innovation.

In the 1970s, the company combated the threat from motorized toys by launching the Lego motor, which could be used to drive countless vehicular contraptions.

More recently, the company has stayed current by introducing a series of themed Lego sets to complement the classic Lego. In recent years, these have included "Knights and Dragons," "Dinosaurs," "Insectoids" and "The Lost World."

The company has also created its own theme parks, with breathtaking Lego models and rides. It has added a UK Legoland in Windsor, to the original Legoland in Denmark.

What has kept the Lego brand strong while other toys have dated, is the constant innovation and freshness. To date, the company has been managed in a way that has kept it young at heart. If this remains the case, the Lego brand will last for as long as children have imagination.

P ut on your blue jeans and there is a strong chance it will be a pair of Levi's. In the 1970s, disenchanted young Communists yearned for a pair of Levi's. They were a black market item in Poland or Czechoslovakia. Levi's symbolized the freedom of the highway, the individualism of Western decadence. They were James Dean. The Marlboro cowboy appeared to wear little else. Levi's remain icons – you know when you have arrived when there is a colorful and expensive coffee table book portraying your role in American culture – and a $100 million ad budget makes sure we don't forget it.

Thanks to such icon status, Levi-Strauss & Co is the world's largest apparel company with revenues of $6 billion (1997). "Next time you're in a Shanghai launderette, or a juke joint in Joliet, or a boardroom in midtown Manhattan, look for us. We'll be a simple, but essential, part of someone's individual style," runs one company ad.

Not only is Levi's a top ranking global brand, it has got there the ethical way. The company has consistently won awards from public bodies and praise from business leaders for its commitment to ethics, values and social responsibility. In a poll of US business leaders, Levi-Strauss was voted the country's most ethical private company – an honor shared with the Merck Corporation, consistently recognized as America's most ethical public company.

At Levi-Strauss, ethics and values are not an afterthought; concepts bolted on to the business when economic success is guaranteed. They are at the core of its culture and are perceived to be key drivers of business success. The company manages its ethics and values commitments with the same degree of care and attention that it devotes to other critical business issues. As with Marks & Spencer in Britain, Robert Bosch in Germany and Tata Industries in India, the company's commitment to good ethics and values was set by its founding family. But, it has successfully transferred the family's personal commitment to ethics, values and social responsibility into its worldwide business ethos and management practices.

The importance of such historical commitment cannot be underestimated. A culture of ethics, values and social responsibility is built over time rather than overnight. Just as the Watsons influenced the culture of IBM so the Haas and Koshland families have influenced the ethics and values of Levi-Strauss. The company has been a family owned business for most of its 140-year history and this connection has been critical in shaping its sense of values and its brand.

From waist-highs to dockers

The original Levi Strauss (1829–1902) came from Bavaria. He arrived in New York in 1847 and worked with his half brothers in their dry goods business. In 1853 Strauss went to San Francisco to set up his own business. His big break came when one of his customers, a Nevada tailor called Jacob Davis, showed him an idea he had for riveting men's trousers. The result was robust and long lasting – suitable if you were a gold prospector or a farmer. Davis needed $68 to file a patent for the design. In 1873 Strauss and Davis patented the riveted trousers or "waist-high overalls" as they were then called. The company prospered – when he died, Levi Strauss's estate was worth the then colossal amount of $6 million.

The first major challenge faced by the company occurred in 1906 when an earthquake followed by a fire destroyed the company's headquarters and two factories. In response, Levi Strauss extended credit to its wholesale customers so they could get back on their feet and back in business. The company carried on paying its employees and a temporary office and showroom was opened to give them some work to do while a new HQ and factory were built.

A similar example was followed by the company during the Great Depression. The then CEO Walter Haas Sr employed workers laying new floors at the company's Valencia Street plant in San Francisco rather than laying them off. Later, the company ensured equal employment opportunities for African Americans in its factories during the 1950s and 1960s when expanding into the southern States. As the business expanded the community involvement tradition developed alongside. Levi-Strauss now draws over 40 percent of its revenues from its international businesses and sources product from over 50 countries worldwide. A quarter of its employees are outside of the US.

Key decades in the development of the company were the 1960s and 1980s. In 1959 the company began exporting to Europe for the first time. In 1966 Levi's ran its first TV ad. The central event of the times, however, was out of the company's control: Woodstock and the Summer of Love. The young soul rebels sat smoking joints wrapped in afghans and, inevitably, wearing jeans. Jeans became the uniform of youth. This has largely remained the case ever since. Punks may have ripped their trousers and covered them in safety pins, but they were still jeans and, most likely, Levi's.

While the 1960s saw Levi's reach international markets and become accepted as youth-wear, the 1970s were a different story. In the 1970s it was successfully prosecuted, under Anti-Trust law in California. In 1971 the company went public. This proved highly unsuccessful. It also brought in a CEO from Playtex who encouraged it into brand extensions. Levi's swimwear, Levi's headgear and Levi's rainwear were among the best forgotten diversions from the main business.

Ups and downs

Between 1980 and 1984, the company's net income fell by over 80 percent. It shut or sold one quarter of its US factories and cut its workforce by 15,000 – nearly one third. "The trust in the company and its leadership in particular was shattered," reflected the man charged with rebuilding it, Robert D. Haas, the great-great grand-nephew of the founder. Haas, an ex-McKinsey consultant, was not without blame – he had been with the company since 1973. He took over as CEO in 1984 and has successfully transmuted the company's benevolent paternalism into a more dynamic, modern approach to managing ethics and values, one which engages employees in the process.

Haas returned the company to private ownership and re-galvanised the company through international expansion and the launch of the hugely successful Dockers casual range. The only major blip was a disastrous attempt at re-engineering.

Ethics remain an integral part of the company. The company published an "aspirations statement" in 1987 which challenges all employees to show leadership in "modeling new behaviors, empowerment, ethical management practices and good communications." The Aspirations Statement also recognizes that people need recognition for their work and positive behavior and commits the company to valuing and make good use of human diversity whether by age, race, sex or ethnic group. It is not decorative. Managers are not judged by economic performance alone. This is a critical message for the importance of these values to the company. Up to 40 percent of management bonuses are decided on performance measures relating to ethics, values and personal style in human relations as set out in the Aspirations Statement and elsewhere.

"We have told our people around the world what we value, and they will hold us accountable," says company president, Peter Jacobi. "Once you do that, it's like letting the genie out of the bottle. You can't go back." Managers obviously like it – turnover among them at the company's San Francisco HQ is a miniscule 1.5 percent annually.[1]

Robert Haas has forcefully argued that an empowered workforce, one sharing the same values and aspirations for the company as managers and owners, will make it a leader in the market. "You can't energize people or earn their support unless the organization has soul," says Haas.

Putting soul back in the brand has only been part of the story. Levi Strauss has launched a number of successful new products. The most notable product development was the launch of the Dockers range in 1986. Dockers became one of the quickest success stories in clothing history.

The channel's the thing

While the product has remained much the same over the decades, what has changed is how Levi's manages and perceives the channels through which it sells its products. Levi's is seeking to reinvent the brand experience. "We are appealing to a broad range of consumers for different wearing occasions in casual wear, and as long as they feel that our products fulfil their psychological needs as well as the product requirements, we've made our mark," says CEO Robert Haas. The psychological experience is the thing – as well as the physical satisfaction of the product. "We are in the comfort business and I don't just mean physical comfort. I mean we are providing psychological comfort – the feeling of security that, when you enter a room of strangers or even work colleagues, you are attired within the band of acceptability. Although obviously what a consumer defines as psychological comfort may vary from sub-segment to sub-segment."[2]

As part of this, Levi-Strauss has developed innovative new delivery systems to consumers. Visit the flagship Levi's store in London's Regent Street and you can climb the stairs and order a pair of customized jeans. Details are fed into a computer and then to Belgium where the jeans are made. They arrive three weeks later complete with a personalized bar code to make reordering straightforward. The ultimate mass marketed product is now available in customized form. This is the age of mass customization and, more precisely, mass *service* customization.

In 1998 Levi's launched Levi's Original Spin which enables customers to design their own jeans using touch screen technology in a special kiosk. "Get your blue jeans here. Be one of the first to build your own unique pair of Levi's jeans" announced the kiosk advertising.

The aim is "customer intimacy." For Levi-Strauss, intimacy with customers is the future of its brand.

A riveting story

- 1847: Bavarian emigrant Levi Strauss arrives in New York.
- 1853: Strauss moves to San Francisco and starts up in business.
- 1873: Strauss and Jacob Davis patent riveted men's trousers.
- 1906: HQ and factory destroyed by earthquake and fire.
- 1920: Levi's set up a factory in Indiana to make "Koveralls" for children. It was the company's first nationally sold product.
- 1940s: American soldiers helpfully wore their Levi's when enjoying R&R in Europe.
- 1959: Levi's exported to Europe for the first time.
- 1961: Levi's exhibited in Paris.
- 1965: Levi-Strauss International and Levi-Strauss Far East established.
- 1966: First Levi's TV ad.
- 1971: Company goes public.
- 1983: Opens its first stores in Europe.
- 1984: Robert Haas becomes CEO.
- 1985: Reverts to private ownership.
- 1986: Dockers brand introduced.
- 1991: Original Levi's stores opened in US.
- 1996: Slates introduced.
- 1998: Downturn in sales sees the company make dramatic cuts.

Notes

1 Sherman, Stratford, "Levi's: As ye sew, so shall ye reap," *Fortune*, May 12, 1997.

2   McGregor, Alexander, "Torn in the USA?" *How to Spend It* supplement, *Financial Times*, May 1998.

I n 1961, the tobacco company RJ Reynolds had reason to feel complacent. Its market share was approaching 35 percent. It was the dominant force in the American cigarette industry. Among those trailing, breathlessly behind – in sixth place – was the Philip Morris company whose market share was less than 10 percent. Executives at RJ Reynolds no doubt lay back in their executive style chairs and inhaled deeply on one of their successful products.

Meanwhile plans were being hatched at Philip Morris. They smacked of desperation. One of its brands was targeted at the female smoker. The bright idea was to re-brand it so that it was targeted at the general market. To make the switch blindingly obvious to consumers, it was decided that the re-branded cigarette would have a cowboy as its resident mascot. The brand was Marlboro, one of the world's most successful and durable brands.

Marlboro is more than a brand. It is an international product, name and image known the world over. Its distinctive red and white colors and its advertising featuring romantic images of the classic American cowboy are universal. Yet, even icons are now facing intensifying competition and competing brands that have little respect for their venerable age and status.

Black Friday

On April 2, 1993, the US tobacco giant Philip Morris cut the price of its branded cigarettes – including Marlboro – by 25 percent. A day earlier, people might have thought the company was joking, but this was deadly serious. Just over a year later, on June 19, 1994, Michael Miles, the man who made the decision, resigned as chairman and chief executive of Philip Morris. The story behind what has become known as Marlboro Friday resounds with many of the vital questions that lie at the heart of branding and brand management in the modern business.

Marlboro and others in the Philip Morris range had suffered from long-term loss of market share to generic (unbranded) cigarettes. (It is worth remembering that Philip Morris also produces the cheaper cigarettes that were undermining Marlboro – but that the profit margins are understandably smaller.) Before Marlboro Friday the unbranded cigarettes had claimed almost 40 percent of the US market. Selling at half the price of Marlboro, the cheaper competitors, along with RJR Nabisco's Camel brand, had sliced Marlboro's US market share from nearly 30 percent to just over 22 percent. Michael Miles decided that something needed to be done.

Miles had been described as "aloof and uncommunicative." *Fortune* had labelled him "a business junkie ... pragmatic, ruthless, focused ... cold blooded."[1] He was also a non-smoker and his experience was in the food side of Philip Morris's massive business empire in which 1993 sales totaled $61 billion. His food-based background, legend would have it, meant that Miles lacked real enthusiasm for the brand and understanding as to the business and what Marlboro stands for. With market share falling, the normal solution would have been an advertising blitz or a small price cut, perhaps both. They might have prodded Marlboro's market share in the right direction.

Miles's solution was more dramatic and unexpected: a massive price cut. Cutting the price of the world's leading cigarette by a fifth to increase flagging market share was a very high-risk gamble indeed. To many commentators, observers and analysts it was a strategy driven by panic rather than by long-term considerations.

As well as making cigarettes cheaper, Marlboro Friday had other wider-ranging implications. In one fell swoop it brought to an end the romantic veneration of brands that had evolved during the 1980s. Instead of secure money-making machines, brands were suddenly unclothed as fallible, potential victims no matter what their size. There was an outbreak of realism – during the 1980s brands had grown, largely in many cases due to premium pricing, fuelled by annual price increases, often up to 15 percent. The succession of price increases had, in many markets, driven customers into the hands of competitors – hence the growth in own-label goods.

Marlboro Friday marked a new – and none too welcoming – dawn. The stock markets responded with disbelief, as they often do when caught totally unprepared. Philip Morris' shares plummeted 23 percent in one day. (In a final insult to Michael Miles, they rose immediately after his departure.)

Miles' strategy was basically straightforward. He recognized that the company could not continue to charge a high premium price for the Marlboro brand – one which was clearly regarded by many consumers as being excessive. Perhaps with an eye to what Compaq had done in PCs, he sought to reduce prices and utilize the immense strength of the brand to drive up market share.

In fact, Miles' strategy worked. In the initial period after Marlboro Friday, Philip Morris shares largely recovered and the company grew its total share of the US tobacco market from 42 percent to 46 percent, with Marlboro alone growing from 22 percent to 27 percent. In July 1994 Philip Morris was able to report a 17.6 percent surge in after-tax profits to $1.23 billion in its second quarter alone – more significant was the fact that this was the first increase in profits recorded since Marlboro Friday. Sales were up by nearly 22 percent in the USA, giving Morris 46.6 percent market share (up five percent) while Marlboro reached a record 28.5 percent – up 6.5 percent.

What eventually finished Miles' career with Philip Morris was his plan to separate the company's two core businesses – tobacco and food and drinks (including Maxwell House, Kraft and Miller beer). This met with opposition from former chairman, Hamish Maxwell, who had masterminded the company's diversification in the 1980s through eye-catching buys such as General Foods, Kraft and Jacobs Suchard.

Again Miles' logic was clear. Maxwell had built up the food side of the company's business in the 1980s when it seemed that tobacco was likely to be a declining and potentially troublesome business to be in. The strategy worked to the extent that the food side of Philip Morris accounted for almost half of its turnover by 1993 – though it was far from being as profitable as tobacco. Miles had actually become part of Morris when it took over Kraft where he was chairman and chief executive. Experienced in the foods business, he was keen to divide the two empires – he was also reacting to the intense anti-smoking lobby in the US and the threat of litigation.

After a six hour board meeting, Miles' plan was rejected. His position made untenable, he left weeks later, to be replaced by two smokers from the tobacco side of Philip Morris' business. In Marlboro country, the smokers still rule the corporate roost.

Note

1   *Fortune*, October 23, 1989.

Mars

When Roald Dahl wrote the childrens' classic *Charlie and the Chocolate Factory* and created the character of the confectionery entrepreneur Willy Wonka, he might have had Forrest Mars, the now retired patriarch of Mars Inc., in mind. Both built their chocolate empires on a passion for quality and secrecy. (For the record, Dahl's book is said to be based on the Cadbury and Rowntree factories in England where spying was rife).

To this day, Forrest Mars, the man who built a $10 billion a year confectionery empire, remains one of the most mysterious figures in the history of corporate America. The brilliant, if guarded, architect of the Mars brand is one of the most private and successful entrepreneurs in the world.

A recent book examines the rivalry between Mars and its chocolate nemesis Hershey.[1] It paints a picture of the American confectionery giants that is as bizarre as anything Dahl could have imagined; a world where industry spies trade in secret recipes and inside information; where paranoid executives are locked in mortal struggle for market share.

Forrest Mars is described as "an autocrat, with brilliant – if sometimes unconventional – management strategies". To an outsider, the secrecy over chocolate recipes, may seem excessive. But the ferocity of competition for confectionery shelf space is real enough.

Today, Mars products are sold in more than 150 countries around the world. The company is run jointly by CEO John Mars and his older brother Forrest Jr., from its headquarters in Virginia at 6885 Elm Street, McLean.

Publicity-shy it may be, but for more than 80 years Mars has been a market leader around the world. In that time the company has created one of the most powerful brands on the planet.

The men from Mars

Franklin C. Mars, the company founder, started selling confectionery in 1902, at the age of 19. By his mid-20s, he had set up a wholesale candy business in Tacoma, in Washington State. A decade or so later, he moved to Minneapolis, where he made butter creams in the family kitchen, which were delivered to shops in the city by Ethel Mars, his wife.

In 1922, the Mar-O-Bar Company was established to make quality confectionery bar products. Today, the name Mars is synonymous with the company's successful products, but in the first year of trading the company made a loss of $6000. Franklin was not easily put off. The following year, the Milky Way bar (known outside the US as the Mars Bar) was introduced and quickly established itself with candy consumers.

This was followed by the Snickers bar (originally called Marathon in Britain), which was launched as a summer product without its familiar chocolate covering.

The company grew so rapidly that it had to move to a larger factory. It became Mars Incorporated, and in 1929 moved to a site just outside Chicago. A year later, the Snickers bar made it first appearance with a chocolate covering.

In 1932, Frank's son, Forrest E. Mars left the US for Britain. He took with him the recipe for the Mars bar, and established his business in a rented factory in Slough. At that time, solid chocolate blocks were popular and the Mars bar with its soft caramel and nougat filling was unique. Made entirely by hand, the Mars bar sold locally for two pence a time.

Word of the remarkable confectionery bars soon spread and Forrest Mars had to double his staff in just six months. The Milky Way bar (UK version) was introduced in 1935, and was followed a few years later by another Mars classic, Maltesers.

Early slogans included "Mars are marvelous" and "There's a meal in a Mars," but the company's enduring catch phrase is "A Mars a day, helps you work, rest and play."

Today, the Mars family – whose wealth is estimated at $10 billion – may reside in the US, but the effects of the formative years in Britain remain. "You want to know why Mars doesn't make any products with peanut butter?" asks a senior Mars executive. "It's because the [Mars] family doesn't eat peanut butter."

Willy Wonka trusts only his faithful workers the Oompa Loompas. Forrest Mars had a similar philosophy. The company, which remains privately owned, has a reputation for treating its employees well and paying above average salaries. It is also highly secretive about its methods, and shuns media attention

Many of those inside the company put its success down to exceptional products and an enlightened management philosophy. The two are closely linked and give the Mars brand a sense of continuity. Mars does not go in for management gimmicks or quick-fix solutions. This sends a message to consumers that the company is not in business for the short term but intends to be around for many years to come.

Status is a dirty word at Mars. Everyone works side by side regardless of rank. No one has a personal secretary, everyone makes his own photocopies and takes his own phone calls. John Mars is probably the only CEO of a major multinational who still clocks in and out every day like a traditional factory worker.

Bureaucracy is anathema. Writing memos is against corporate policy. Corporate HQ in McLean employs just 51 people, including John, Forrest Jr and Jackie.

Pay is tied directly to the company's business performance. If profits soar, "associates" are eligible for bonuses equal to five, ten or even fifteen weeks' salary. On the other side, if profits drop, so does their income.

Cleanliness is a company obsession. The company's proud boast is that at any given time the acceptable level of bacteria on a Mars factory floor is less than the average level in a domestic household sink. Any hint of contamination is enough to shut down production for hours.

Quality is a compulsion. Every year, millions of M&Ms, the chocolate filled shells that are one of the company's leading products, are rejected because the "M" they are marked with isn't in quite the right place. A pinhole in a Snickers is reason enough to destroy an entire batch. On such perfectionism an empire has been built.

Note

1   Brenner, Joel Glenn, *The Chocolate Wars: Inside the Secret Worlds of Mars & Hershey*, HarperCollins Business, 1999.

McDonald's

T he two McDonald brothers – Dick and Maurice (known by all as Mac) – opened up a restaurant in San Bernardino, CA in 1940. It was nothing unusual – a barbecue and car-hop place. As they became more experienced, the McDonalds realized that their customers wanted food in a hurry. They didn't want to be waited on necessarily. They just wanted their food quickly. So, in December 1948, Dick and Mac moved into fast food. Their new restaurant was topped by a large neon sign proclaiming that Speedee the Chef worked there.

It wasn't a particularly sophisticated sort of place. Dick came up with the idea of a couple of arches to represent the letter M and put tiles (red and white) on the walls so that they could be easily cleaned. Customers could drive in and place their order at the first window. The choice wasn't great, but by the time they'd driven to the next window, their order was ready. The customers loved it. It was cheap and easy – a hamburger cost 15 cents, a malt drink 20 cents and a pack of fries 10 cents.

The customers flocked and the McDonald brothers expanded their empire. Eventually they had eight restaurants all following the same formula. (Only one now still stands – the third in east Los Angeles.) Their success came to the attention of Ray Kroc (1902–84), a kitchen equipment salesman who sold marketing rights to milkshake mixers. In 1954 Kroc bought the American franchise to McDonald's for $2.7 million and, in 1961, bought the world rights. The rest is history. As the McDonald brothers stepped back into branding mythology, Kroc took over the world.

Kroc brought dynamism combined with homespun business philosophy – "Persistence and determination alone are omnipotent"; "If a corporation has two executives who think alike, one is unnecessary"; or try Kroc on helping your neighbor: "If I saw a competitor drowning I'd put a live fire hose in his mouth." It worked. The 100th

McDonald's opened in 1959; the first outside the US in 1967; and, in 1990, the last bastion fell when McDonald's opened up in Moscow. Russians couldn't buy anything in their supermarkets, but could admire the efficiency of capitalism at work as the entire foreign community in Moscow ate at McDonald's.

The ninth restaurant in the McDonald's chain – and Kroc's first – was in Des Plaines, Illinois. McDonald's HQ is located nearby at Oak Brook. Today, McDonald's has 24,500 restaurants in 114 countries around the world. A staggering 38 million people eat at a McDonald's restaurant on every single day of the week.

Beautiful buns

The formula is astonishingly universal (and international sales account for 60 percent of McDonald's earnings): limited choice, quick service and clean restaurants. While McDonald's is successful across the world there is nothing particularly original or innovative about what it does. You don't have to be one of the Le Roux brothers to serve up a tasty cheeseburger. Instead McDonald's does the simple things well. A McDonald's restaurant in Nairobi, Kenya looks much the same as one in Warsaw, Poland or Battle Creek, Michigan. (Even so, there are some allowances for local tastes – lamb burgers in India and kosher burgers in Israel.) It is, McDonald's proclaims, the "most successful food service organization in the world."

Henry Ford mastered mass product production; McDonald's has mastered mass service production. It has done so through strict adherence to simple beliefs. Quality, cleanliness and uniformity are the basis of the McDonald's brand. Kroc was an obsessive about these issues. "It requires a certain kind of mind to see beauty in a hamburger bun," he reflected. He was right – no-one else manages to do the simple things as well. In effect, the very uniformity of the brand is the crucial differentiating factor.

It worked for decades. But, the 1990s have been years of doubt for McDonald's. The juggernaut has not exactly hit the buffers, but it has scored some notable own goals – the pointless UK libel case which saw the company in protracted and expensive argument with two individuals who ran rings around the giant; flop new products such as the Arch Deluxe and unsuccessful promotions like the 55 cent burger. Burger King has enjoyed recent years.

In 1998, the company appointed a new CEO, Jack Greenberg, the first McDonald's chief who has not served his time as a hamburger flipper. Greenberg is clearly well tutored in fashionable management theory – "I don't have all the answers, and that's powerful," he says. "I have the self-confidence to surround myself with strong people and take the time to listen. A feedback environment is the only way to attract the best people"[1] – but faces a surprisingly sizeable task in breathing life into what is now a $33 billion corporation.[2]

In many ways the problems now faced by McDonald's were tackled by many other brands some years ago. McDonald's, for example, is heavily centralized. Its cadre of middle and senior managers tend to have come up through the ranks. Different voices have been notable by their absence. It has also generally ignored segmenting its markets – "The old model of just telling people what to do was exactly the right model for a long, long time," says Greenberg. "Now we need a different approach to managing that pays more attention to different market segments."[3]

The other vital missing ingredient is innovation. McDonald's has proved an unimaginative and generally unsuccessful innovator. "We have been taking much too long to develop an idea and get it to the market, then too long to decide whether we want to do it or not," admits Greenberg.[4] While Greenberg accepts that it must change, whether such a huge organization with such a strong culture can do so remains open to question.

More positively, McDonald's still possesses the all-conquering self-esteem of a global powerhouse. Its publicity material notes with some regret that "On any day, even as the market leader, McDonald's serves less than one percent of the world's population." There are always more mouths to feed.

Notes

1   Machan, Dyann, "Polishing the golden arches," *Forbes*, June 15, 1998.

2   McDonald's 1997 sales were $33,638.3 million with over 61 percent from outside the US.

3   Machan, Dyann, "Polishing the golden arches," *Forbes*, June 15, 1998.

4   Tomkins, Richard, "A mission to buff up the golden arches," *Financial Times*, September 3, 1998.

McKinsey & Co.

Insiders in the consultancy McKinsey & Company always call it *The Firm*. There is an assumption that when it comes to management consultancy, McKinsey operates on a different plain – where the bills are larger, the hours longer, standards higher, the results better and the people brighter. McKinsey consultants like to think of themselves as the movie stars of the business world. They dazzle you not with their expensive coiffures, but with their intellects.

The Firm is more than a mere consultancy. It is an ethos. Staid suits and professional standards. Clean-cut and conservative. It is obsessively professional and hugely successful; a slick, well-oiled financial machine. McKinsey is one of the great brands of the professional service industry.

Eulogies to McKinsey are easy to find. Most examinations of the world of management consultants stop at the company's portals and pay homage. "The most well-known, most secretive, most high-priced, most prestigious, most consistently successful, most envied, most trusted, most disliked management consulting firm on earth," is how *Fortune* described McKinsey.[1] Tom Peters prefers to observe that "McKinsey has a stratospheric belief in itself."[2] There is no hyperbole in Peters' observation. It is simple, matter of fact.

McKinsey is driven by belief; faith in the McKinsey doctrine. Self-effacing modesty is not on the agenda. Modesty and McKinsey are as comfortable with each other as a Carmelite nun would be exchanging small talk with Arnold Schwarzenegger.

Hat culture

However, apart from its somewhat overblown aspirations, what is so special about McKinsey? After all, it is not the oldest consultancy company. Arthur D Little can trace its lineage back to the 1880s. Nor is McKinsey the biggest consultancy company in the world – Andersen Consulting dwarfs it in terms of revenues and numbers of consultants (but not, significantly, in revenue per consultant). McKinsey is special because it likes to think of itself as the best and has developed a self-perpetuating aura that it is unquestionably the best.

McKinsey's faith in its own brilliance is part of a unique corporate culture. Its creation can largely be attributed to a single man, Marvin Bower who joined the business in the 1930s. Bower's heritage and the McKinsey corporate culture are safeguarded by the company's rules which mean that in the spring every three years McKinsey's senior partners – over 150 known as directors – vote in an open ballot to determine the managing director. Admirably democratic, the election of a McKinsey managing director has, somewhat appropriately, more in common with the selection of a new Pope than the usual machinations of choosing a CEO.

Indeed, McKinsey constantly asserts its difference. "My vision was to provide advice on managing to top executives and to do it with the professional standards of a leading law firm," said Bower.[3] Consequently, McKinsey is always The Firm rather than a corporation tainted by its obvious commercial *raison d'être*. Its consultants are "associates." McKinsey has "engagements" rather than mere jobs and is a "practice" rather than a business. It is laden with pretension, but generates money in a thoroughly unpretentious manner.

Bower's gospel was that the interests of the client should precede increasing the company's revenues. If you looked after the client, the profits would look after themselves. (High charges are not a means to greater profits, according to McKinsey, but a simple and effective means of ensuring that clients take McKinsey seriously.) Bower's other rules were that consultants should keep quiet about the affairs of clients; should tell the truth and be prepared to challenge the client's opinion; and should only agree to do work which is both necessary and which they could do well. To this he added a few idiosyncratic twists such as insisting that all McKinsey consultants wore hats – except, for some reason, in the San Francisco office – and long socks. The sight of a consultant's flesh was deemed too much for clients to bear.

Working at McKinsey is no cozy sinecure. Preventing managers taking dumb options is not easy. Expectations are enormous, as Tom Peters discovered. Only the best will do. McKinsey's traditional hunting grounds are the leading business schools – Harvard, Stanford, Chicago, MIT's Sloan, Kellogg at NorthWestern, Wharton and France's Insead.

McKinsey's recruits are WASPs almost to a man and men they almost always are. The bright, energetic MBA graduates are thrown into the fray immediately. A McKinsey consultant is reckoned to peak at around 45 (Lou Gerstner, now of IBM, holds the record at 31 of being the youngest person ever to become a senior partner) and, by the time they reach their 50s, they are slowing down, cutting out the exhaustive committee work and retiring at 60. They work hard and are paid very well.

Inevitably, many fail to stand the heat and leave or are speedily dispatched to lesser lights in the consultancy world (or to the real world of running companies). The consultants know where they stand. McKinsey's recruitment brochure says: "If a consultant ceases to progress with The Firm, or is ultimately unable to demonstrate the skills and qualities required of a principal, he or she is asked to leave McKinsey. This 'up or out' policy is applied throughout The Firm. It is a way of ensuring that we continue to maintain the high-performance people we must retain, and maintain our ability to provide superior client service"[4] Its reputation and the rewards are such that McKinsey has around 50,000 applications every year from which it recruits around 550 new consultants.

Notes

1   Huey, John, "How McKinsey does it," *Fortune*, November 1, 1993.

2   Interview with authors.
3   Huey, John, "How McKinsey does it," *Fortune*, November 1, 1993.
4   Hecht, Françoise, "The firm walks tall," *Eurobusiness*, February 1995.

"Oh Lord, won't you buy me a Mercedes-Benz," Janis Joplin wailed, "My friends all have Porsches and I want to make amends." The appeal of the Mercedes-Benz brand was immortalized in a song. People understood: they wanted one as well.

At Daimler-Benz, where the illustrious brand resides, they put it slightly differently. "At Daimler-Benz the name 'Mercedes-Benz' is considered a synonym for the production of high-quality and innovative vehicles," the company's web-site proclaims with due solemnity.

But Daimler was not averse to a posthumous endorsement from Joplin. The company used her rendition in a recent advertising campaign. This is the magic of the Mercedes brand: it is a premium quality automobile brand that appeals to a wide range of people. The famous three-pointed star logo is one of the most widely recognized logos the world has ever known.

In a 1997 analysis of the leading global brands, the branding experts Interbrand, ranked Mercedes-Benz seventh, ahead of both Levi Strauss and Marlboro. The consultancy noted: "For many, Mercedes-Benz is the ultimate in status brands, embodying safety, heritage, and longevity."

The marque also has that special quality you can't quite put your finger on; an aura that surrounds the world's top brands. Impossible to describe, Mercedes drivers say, it is something you feel when you sit behind the wheel: a sense of having reached the pinnacle of human achievement in a certain field; a sense of having arrived; that cars really don't get any better than this.

At least, that's what Mercedes would like us to feel. And the company does everything it can to make that intangible experience real for the people who buy its cars.

Learning to drive

The origins of the Daimler-Benz group go back to 1883. In that year Karl Benz, Max Rose and Friedrich Wilhelm Esslinger founded Benz & Co. in the German town of Mannheim. The first motor cars took to the roads in 1886. The Benz & Co. designed car made its debut in July. At around the same time, Gottlieb Daimler, working separately, also carried out trials with his design for a motor carriage.

By the late 1880s, the brand's identity was already starting to emerge. A Mercedes advertisement dating from 1888 or 1889 may be the first ever for a motor vehicle. It sang the praises of the Benz three-wheeler invented in 1885 and considered by Mercedes fans to be the first true automobile. Only a handful of the wondrous machine were built. Mass production would have to wait until Henry Ford arrived on the scene.

In 1890, Daimler founded the Daimler-Motoren-Gesellschaft (DMG) in the town of Bad Cannstatt just outside Stuttgart. It is claimed that the design of the first fully functional vehicle engine in America, built in Hartford, Connecticut, was based on drawings produced by Daimler.

Daimler's sons suggested the star be used as a trademark. Their father had once sent his wife a postcard with a star marking out the house where he was boarding in Deutz. He wrote on the card: "One day this star will shine down on my work." In 1909, a trademark was taken out on the star. Its three points symbolize the three branches of motorization: on land, on water and in the air.

In the depression in Germany that followed the end of World War I, the Benz and Daimler companies were hit by hard times and forced to diversify into other consumer goods such as typewriters and bicycles.

The prevailing economic climate and the over supply of vehicle manufacturers also encouraged alliances. By combining forces, companies stood a better chance of gaining sufficient market share to be viable. In 1924, Daimler and Benz formed an association of common interest, marketing their cars under the now famous Mercedes-Benz trade name.

The Mercedes-Benz brand established itself as the classic fusion of German engineering and stylish design. Unlike other German marques the best models brought together the beauty of the car designer's art with the reliability and longevity of solid no-nonsense mechanics. Mercedes were built to last. The way they looked and felt gave buyers confidence that the premium price was money well spent.

The glory days of Daimler-Benz were the 1960 and 1970s when the classy cars redefined the luxury market. Such was the prestige of any vehicle that bore the three-pointed star on its hood that price was not an issue. By the 1980s, however, the US automobile industry was in disarray, and competition in Europe was becoming more intense. Not only were other European marques including BMW, looking to close the gap with Mercedes, the Japanese in the shape of Toyota's Lexus – a Mercedes wannabee if there ever was one - were making a concerted effort to muscle into the luxury car market.

Some luxury brands went under or, like the British marques Jaguar and Rolls Royce, found themselves pushed from pillar to post in a desperate search for a new home. For a time, the leviathan Daimler-Benz seemed impervious to the crisis engulfing the European car market, but eventually it, too, found itself struggling against the tide of competition.

The business press briefly hailed the company's charismatic chairman Jurgen Schempp as Germany's Jack Welch, the CEO credited with saving General Electric. He was dubbed Neutron Jurgen as he fought to slim down the monolithic Daimler machine into something more economically viable and fleet of foot. But even with a brand as powerful as Mercedes-Benz, the company could not survive alone. The question was who to couple its carriage to? The answer: a re-invented and greatly improved Chrysler in a deal codenamed Operation Gamma.

The deal was sealed in early 1998, with a $40 billion merger of the two legendary auto brands. It combined Mercedes' brand muscle in the luxury car market with Chrysler's share of the volume market (attempts by Mercedes to crack the volume market with it's own cheaper Mercedes branded offering called the A-Type had run into problems).

The deal was a reality check for many in the car industry. It underlined the dramatic game of survival being played out among the world's leading manufacturers. An editorial in *Fortune* observed: "The result, the largest industrial marriage in history, takes what had been the world's number 6 car company, Chrysler, and stuffs it into the trunk of erstwhile number 15 Daimler-Benz to produce the planet's fifth biggest automobile concern."

Valued at around $40 billion, the new company has 400,000 employees and is expected to generate around $130 billion in sales. Mercedes-Benz purists may mourn the passing of the company's German identity. But the deal guarantees the survival of one of the most famous brands in the world.

*M*icrosoft

T|he arrival of the Microsoft brand represents a major change in the business world. For the first time ever, branding the intangible – a computer program called MS-DOS – was more powerful than traditional physical brands. With Microsoft Bill Gates branded brainpower.

Founded in the mid-1970s by Gates and his long-time friend Paul Allen, by the second half of the 1980s, Microsoft had become the darling of Wall Street. From a share price of $2 in 1986, Microsoft stock soared to $105 by first half of 1996, making Gates a billionaire and many of his colleagues millionaires.

But the rise in Microsoft's share price also signaled the end of the old world order. There were technology brands before Microsoft, but they were on the hardware side. IBM, Digital Equipment, Motorola, were all technology brands. In Detroit, the brands of General Motors, Ford and Chrysler were based on their technological leadership, as was General Electric. What all had in common was that they put their logos on technology that customers could see and touch – even if they didn't understand how it worked. Microsoft was different. It put its brand on something called an "operating system."

Without an IBM box, the Microsoft brand was meaningless: at least, that's what IBM thought when they signed Bill Gates to supply the operating system for the company's first PC. At a fateful meeting with IBM in 1980 the future of the entire computer industry – and arguably the entire business world – took an unexpected turn. Executives from Big Blue signed a contract with a small Seattle-based software firm to develop the operating system for its first PC. They thought they were simply saving time by outsourcing a non-core activity to a small contractor. After all, they were in the computer hardware business; where the real money and power lay. You could brand a box. You couldn't brand an operating system. But they were wrong.

To some commentators the whole business world changed in the early 1990s when the market valuation of Microsoft – which owned little more than a few buildings in Redmond, Washington, and the Microsoft brand – exceeded that of General Motors – with all its physical asset, factories, components and inventory. On 16 September 1998, the market valuation of Microsoft passed that of the mighty GE, to become America's biggest company with a market value of $262 billion. The intangible brainpower brand had overtaken the physical.

Tough love

Despite its enormous success, customers appear to have a curious love–hate relationship with the Microsoft brand. The brand dominates the software market, but seems at times to be the target of as much distrust as peace of mind. Microsoft's brand is a victim of the company's own success. It shows what can happen if a brand is perceived to have become too powerful.

People are equally split about Bill Gates. To some in Microsoft, he is a mystical, almost religious figure, while to others in the industry he is the Antichrist. Both views are outrageous, but underline just how powerful his influence is. (With all the hullabaloo about alleged abuse of monopoly power, it is easy to forget that back in the 1970s, IBM, too, was the target of anti-trust investigations. Yet, memory fades. Today, we have come to regard Big Blue as almost saintly compared to Microsoft. Such is the nature of power – we fear most what we understand least.)

Since the early days of Microsoft, Gates has pursued his vision of "a computer on every desk and in every home." (Interestingly, the original slogan was "a computer on every desk in every home, running Microsoft software," but the last part is often left off these days as it makes some people uncomfortable). Recent history has given the company good reason to soften what many perceive as an aggressive message.

More recently, Microsoft has shifted its brand positioning to reflect the "enabling role" of software. "Where do you want to go today?", its best known slogan, is in fact a natural follow on from "a personal computer on every desk in every home." In one sense the PC revolution has been won, and now the new battleground is for the imagination of consumers.

Looking back now, the spread of personal computers from the office into the home seems almost inevitable. Hindsight is a wonderful thing. Foresight, however, is much more lucrative, as Gates has shown. It is important to remember, too, that the ubiquitous screens and keyboards that we all take for granted today were the stuff of science fiction just a couple of decades ago. Back in the 1960s when futurists in America tried to predict the trends that were likely to shape society in the rest of the century they completely missed the rise of the PC.

That Bill Gates alone was responsible for putting the PC in homes and offices all over the world is untrue, any more than Henry Ford was responsible for the rise of the automobile. What the two had in common, however, was the vision to see what was possible, and to play a pivotal role in making that vision a reality.

Gates set about achieving his vision by transforming Microsoft into a major player in the computer industry and using its dominant position to create a platform for the huge growth in applications. What Gates realized very early on was that in order for his vision to succeed it was essential that an industry standard be created. He knew, too, that whoever got there first would have a major opportunity to stamp their own authority on the computing industry.

Microsoft clinched the deal to supply the operating system for IBM. Gates was lucky. But had the same opportunity fallen to one of his Silicon Valley peers, the outcome might have been very different. In Bill Gates, IBM had picked the one man who would not fumble the ball. On such moments does history turn.

What IBM couldn't see, Gates saw very clearly. The world of computing was on the brink of a major change – what the management theorists like to call a paradigm change. Gates understood, in a way that the old IBM guard could not, that software and not hardware was the key to the future. He knew, too, that the muscle of IBM, the market leader, would be required to establish a common standard, or platform, for software applications. That platform would be Q-DOS – an existing operating system that Gates bought for $50,000 from another company – renamed MS-DOS by Microsoft. But even Gates could not have imagined just how lucrative the deal would be for Microsoft.

Bill Gates was too bright not to realize that if he played his cards right, his operating system MS-DOS could become the industry standard. At that time, the operating system itself was just one of several on the market.

Many inside the computer industry felt at that time that from a purely technical perspective MS-DOS had some serious drawbacks. Apple was already established as the provider of choice for desktop computers. Apple's founders had brought new attitude and culture to the computer business. The Apple brand was streets ahead of Microsoft: both in image terms and in terms of perceived quality.

Apple's machines were popular because they were simpler to operate and fun to use. The company had yet to develop the famous icon-based Apple Macintosh operating system, but the signs were already there that the people at Apple were ahead of the game.

But Gates had an important ally. Ironically, it was the muscle of the IBM brand behind his operating system that gave the Microsoft brand its power. Big Blue had dominated the mainframe business for years and, somewhat belatedly, was preparing to enter the PC market. The credibility of the IBM name would be crucial in the battle ahead. Gates judged rightly that the best opportunity of establishing an industry standard other than one based around the Apple system lay with the arrival in the PC market of the world's most trusted computer manufacturer. For many years, IBM's proud boast was that "no one ever got fired for buying an IBM." At that time, it had a reputation for dependability unmatched in the computer world. The IBM PC was bound to take a big slice of the market for desktop computers.

The fact that IBM-badged machines were about to flood the market also meant that the operating system they used would be catapulted into first or second place. Every single PC shipped by IBM would have MS-DOS installed. For Microsoft it was the perfect Trojan Horse. Every IBM badged PC that landed on a desk gave a free ride to the Microsoft operating system that lay hidden inside. This was Bill Gates' amazing piece of luck. But what happened next goes a long way to explaining why Bill Gates and not Steve Jobs, or some other Silicon Valley entrepreneur, is now the richest man in the world.

New rules for the branding game

In the old world, companies protected their brands by maintaining control. This is what Apple attempted to do by refusing to allow its products to be cloned. Apple took the view that the only way to ensure the quality of its products was to try to retain control of everything. Later this included its proprietary Macintosh operating system. For years, the company resolutely refused to licence its Apple Mac operating system to other manufacturers. This meant that anyone who wanted the user-friendly Apple operating system had to buy an Apple computer. It was a strategy that seemed to make sense – but only by the old rules of the game. The problem for Apple was that in terms of business model and strategic vision, it was only one generation on from the hardware dinosaur IBM.

What Gates understood that Apple did not was that the rules were different for intangible brands. By the late 1970s, Microsoft was already licensing its software to a variety of customers. In 1977, Gates supplied software for Tandy, but it also licensed BASIC 6502 to Apple for the Apple II Computer. Microsoft went on to work with many of the other leading computer companies. This suited Bill Gates' purposes perfectly. Microsoft was already beginning to set the industry standard with its software. It was this strategy that he continued with MS-DOS.

In the early 1980s, Gates masterminded Microsoft's movement from a developer of programming languages to a diversified software company producing everything from operating systems such as Windows to applications like Word and Excel, as well as programming tools. In the process he transformed the computer industry – and created the greatest of the intangible brands.

How IBM fumbled its PC brand

IBM was late off the mark with the PC. The company that dominated the mainframe computer business failed to recognize the importance – and the threat presented – by the rise of the personal computer. By the time Big Blue decided to enter the PC market in 1980, Apple, which had pioneered the desktop computer, had become a $100 million business.

Frank Cary, IBM chairman at the time, ordered his people to produce an IBM-badged PC by August 1981. Already in catch-up mode, the IBMers put in charge of the project made two fundamental technical errors. Both mistakes came from a single decision to go outside the company for the two critical elements of the new machine – the microprocessor that would be at the heart of the new PC and the operating system. Intel agreed to supply the chips and a small relatively unknown software company based in Seattle agreed to supply the operating system.

The launch of the IBM PC was initially a commercial success. But the company ended up giving away most of the profits from its PC business to its two partners. Under the initial contract between IBM and Microsoft, Big Blue agreed to fund most of the development costs of MS-DOS, but only Microsoft was allowed to licence the system to third parties. This was the killer clause.

As the PC industry exploded, thousands of new competitors entered the market. Virtually all of them ended up using MS-DOS, and paying Bill Gates for the privilege. But IBM's mistakes didn't end there. When it recognized its initial error, IBM failed to renegotiate the licensing contract or to break with

---

Microsoft. Even more mystifying, senior managers at IBM killed an internally developed operating system that could have broken Gates' stranglehold on the PC market.

More than a decade later, IBM was still manufacturing more PCs than any other company, but its personal systems division was losing money. The only companies making large profits in the highly competitive PC business were the suppliers of the microchips and operating systems. To this day, the computing industry is dominated by two brands: Intel and Microsoft.

I n the ninth century Persians were fond of a drink called *qahwa*. A version of the drink was tried out by Louis XIV. His reaction is not known. Today, coffee is enjoyed by hundreds of millions of people across the world. The staple of this market is powdered coffee and, in this huge international business, there is one brand which remains globally renowned: Nescafé. Every second of every day it is calculated that 3000 cups of the world's leading coffee brand are consumed. (Soluble nugget: 28 percent of Americans have coffee as part of their breakfast.)

The development of Nescafé, the first water-soluble coffee, took research scientists at Nestlé's laboratories in Vevey, Switzerland eight long years. In 1930 the Brazilian Coffee Institute got in touch with the then Nestlé chief, Louis Dapples. Brazil had a sizeable coffee surplus. There was an awful lot of coffee in Brazil and it was anxious to explore ways to sell it more successfully. Nestlé got to work, but it was not until 1937 that its scientists were able to bellow the Swiss equivalent of Eureka as they came up with their version of powdered coffee. Qahwa it wasn't; hugely popular it remains.

The new product was rushed quickly to market after its discovery. It was immediately popular. During World War 2, the entire output of the company's US plant – in excess of one million cases – was reserved for military use. The War saw demand for Nescafé go through the roof – Nestlé's total sales increased from $100 million to $225 million. (It is interesting that the War had such an impact on branding – Coca-Cola cemented its place in the American psyche, troops consumed Heinz soup and were warmed by Nescafé.)

The parent of all coffees

The creator of Nescafé was the brand giant Nestlé. With 489

factories throughout the world, the company sells a plethora of brands to over 100 countries.

The origins of Nestlé can be traced back to 1867. It was then that the Swiss merchant, chemist and inventor, Henri Nestlé, invented a nutritious product for infants whose mothers were unable to breastfeed them. The product was named Farine Lactée Nestlé. Nestlé also came up with a logo for his business – a simple combination of the "nest" in his surname and its association with maternity and comfort. On such simple notions was an empire built.

In 1874, the company was bought from its founder by Jules Monnerat who took the company into the condensed milk market. The business quickly gained an international dimension. In 1898 Nestlé bought a Norwegian condensed milk company. Before long the company had plants in the US, UK, Germany and Spain. It later merged with first the Anglo-Swiss Condensed Milk Company (long its arch-rival) and then Peter, Cailler, Kohler, Chocolat Suisses. In 1907 the company began manufacturing in Australia and built warehouses in Singapore, Hong Kong and India. A further post-war merger with Alimentana brought Maggi seasoning and soups into the Nestlé empire.

In the post-war years, the company sealed its position as a giant of the food industry. From 1950 to 1959, sales of instant coffee nearly tripled and, from 1960 to 1974, they quadrupled. Nestlé's total sales doubled twice in the 15 years after the war. Innovations such as freeze drying helped its expansion – and led to the introduction of the Taster's Choice brand of instant coffee in 1966.

The series of mergers and acquisitions has continued ever since. Nestlé acquired Crosse & Blackwell, Findus, Libby's and Stouffer's. In 1974 it became a major shareholder in the French cosmetics group L'Oréal. The only other significant departure to its core business was the acquisition of Alcon Laboratories in Fort Worth, Texas, a pharmaceutical company specializing in eye care during the 1970s. More standard acquisitions have been Chambourcy (1979); Carnation (for $3 billion in 1985); Rowntree Mackintosh (1988); Buitoni-Perugina (1988); Perrier (1992) and Spillers (1998).

This leaves Nestlé as the largest food company in the world

with 225,000 employees spread throughout the world making and selling over 8500 products. Its sales exceed $50 billion.

Now that's what I call progress

- 1867: Henri Nestlé invents Farine Lactée Nestlé.
- 1875: Milk chocolate invented by Daniel Peter.
- 1881: Fruit pastilles and fruit gums introduced by Rowntree.
- 1883: Dried soups and bullion cubes invented by Julius Maggi.
- 1933: Milo first introduced.
- 1937: Kit Kat, Smarties and Rolo introduced.
- 1938: Nescafé invented.
- 1952: Nestlé Quik introduced.

The Nestlé empire

Soluble coffee
- Nescafé
- Taster's Choice
- Ricoré
- Ricoffy

Roast and ground coffee
- Hills Bros
- MJB
- Bonka
- Zoégas
- Loumidis

Mineral water
- Perrier
- Contrex
- Vittel

- Quézac
- Arrowhead
- Poland Spring
- Buxton
- Vera
- Blaue Quellen
- Calistoga
- Santa Maria
- San Pellegrino

Other beverages
- Nesquick
- Nescau
- Nestea
- Milo
- Carnation
- Libby's
- Caro

And the rest
Dairy products – includes Milkmaid
Breakfast cereals
Coffee creamers – Coffee-mate
Instant foods and dietetic products – including Lactogen
Culinary products – Maggi, Libby's, etc.
Frozen foods – Findus, etc.
Ice cream – Frisco, etc.
Chocolate and confectionery – After Eight, Rolo, Aero, etc.
Pet care – Friskies, etc.
Ophthalmological products – Alcon

F or years Nike's "Just do it" slogan seemed to sum up its whole approach to business. Between 1995 and the first half of 1997, the sports shoe company with the distinctive swoosh logo sprinted from $4.8 billion to $9.2 billion in sales, capturing almost half of the US sports shoe market. At the same time, it continued its expansion around the globe. Since then growth has slowed.

Nike made its name – and much of its money – in basketball and America's jogging boom, both markets that are now saturated. After a hiccup in 1993–4, the company realigned itself – "We decided we're a sports company, not just a shoe company," said CEO Phil Knight.[1]

The new view of itself translated into advertising and sponsorship deals aimed at a wider sports audience. In particular the company promoted a message that we can all be athletes in our own way and at our own level. Product association was critical to the brand strategy.

In 1997, Nike spent an incredible $5.6 billion on marketing, including $4 billion on sponsorship for individual athletes – Tiger Woods and Michael Jordan are two of Nike's key stars. But with its traditional sports of basketball and jogging running out of puff, the company is looking for other sports fields to play on. To achieve Knight's stated goal of a turnover of $2 billion by 2002, the company has targeted soccer as one of its core sports

In the 1998 soccer World Cup hosted by the eventual winners France, it sponsored Brazilian star Ronaldo, Maldini of Italy and England's Sheringham and Scholes. The company also shelled out $400 million for a ten-year deal with Brazil and another $120 million to the US Soccer Federation to sponsor the American team – figuring the sport has to explode there some time.

The brand's massive advertising spend concentrates on a passion for sport. This has gradually evolved into a metaphor for the aspirations consumers have. Recently, Nike has experimented with a new slogan to augment, but not replace its classic "Just do it." The new slogan is "I can."

Nike's starting blocks

Nike is based in Beaverton, Oregon. Its verdant headquarters near the city of Portland reflect its obsession with sport. CEO Knight views his empire from an office in the John McEnroe building. Such fanaticism is in keeping with a company that began life designing shoes for serious athletes.

Knight launched the company in 1964 with Bill Bowerman, his former track coach at the University of Oregon. The idea for the company came from an MBA project when Knight was at business school at Stanford. Knight believed that by importing shoes made using cheap labor in Japan he could undercut the market leader Adidas. He started with running shoes. But one morning Bowerman had a better idea.

According to Nike folklore the sports coach made an outsole by pouring a rubber compound into a waffle iron. Sports shoe technology would never be the same again. Nike was ready to break away from the pack.

Its thoroughbred pedigree still lends kudos to the brand with aspiring sports stars. Over the years, Nike also cultivated a highly competitive management style which mirrors the spirit of sportsmen and women on the field.

The company went public in 1980. Since then, market capitalization has increased by over $12 billion – from $386 million to $13 billion. On a $100 shoe, the manufacturer's profit is around $20 to $25.

More recently, the mighty Nike brand has looked less surefooted. Sales dipped by 8 percent in the third quarter of 1997, and the company was left with piles of inventory in its warehouses. The company has had knock-backs before. In the mid-1980s Knight tied the company in knots with a misguided expansion plan, and sales also tripped up in 1994.

But in recent times Nike has also experienced other problems. On 18 October 1997 pressure groups in the US organized a series of demonstrations worldwide against Nike's use of cheap labor in developing economies. Allegations of subsistence-level pay rates, worker intimidation and the use of child labor, which have dogged Nike for several years, culminated in protests in 50 US cities and 11 countries.

Nike reacted to the criticisms with a range of defensive measures designed to refute the claims while also protecting the company's public image. It joined Apparel Industry Partnership, a new group of clothing manufacturers that hopes to eradicate the use of sweatshops by enforcing an industry-wide code of conduct in their overseas factories.

It also severed its relationship with some of its contractors in Indonesia because they did not adhere to Nike's code of conduct and introduced a system of penalties for other factories failing to meet all of the company's standards.

Nike bashing, however, remained a popular sport. Garry Trudeau also lambasted the company in his Doonesbury cartoon strip, and the film *The Big One* featured Knight in its critical examination of corporate America. The company was also accused of treading on toes as it tried to push its way into the soccer market.

The 1998 World Cup involved more than just a clash of playing styles. France '98 brought the marketing teams of Nike and the resurgent European sports shoe brand Adidas into a penalty shoot-out for the biggest prize in soccer – $4.5 billion worth of sportswear sales. Nose to nose were two new products. Adidas had its new Predator Accelerator boot, while leading Nike's counter attack was its Mercurial boot – "genuinely designed" by the Brazilian star Ronaldo.

The tussle illustrated the approach that has made Nike such a formidable brand. "Those Nike guys call it war, we call it competition," observed an Adidas spokesman. A Nike manager preferred to see it as a sporting contest: "Emotionally, Nike executives are like top sportsman – very focused, very determined, hardworking … They want to win."

"Our hope is that Ronaldo plays in the World Cup Final and scores a goal … wearing our boots." In the event, Ronaldo did play in the final – a mysteriously disappointing appearance that almost caused a riot. He did not look like scoring. Brazil was roundly beaten by the host nation France. (It was also suggested that Nike had somehow put pressure on Brazil to include their star player despite the fact that he was obviously not fully fit.)

"Just do it," however, does not easily translate into French – the result is the French slogan "Ta vie est à toi" – your life is your own. What does translate is the Nike brand essence, which is all about passion for sport.

State-of-the-art sneaker technology

- 1979: The Tailwind – the first shoe to feature Nike-Air cushioning.
- 1983: The Pegasus.
- 1985: The Epic.
- 1987: The Air Max.
- 1991: The Air 180.
- 1993: The Air Max.
- 1994: Air Max 2.
- 1997: Zoom Air.
- 1998: Air Zoom Citizen.

Beware impostors

Copy cat brands are now two-a-penny and not just in the markets of Singapore or the Far East. Today's top seller is tomorrow's bootleg:

- *Ouzo 12* becomes Ouzo 21 – in Greece there is only one brand of ouzo worth drinking (and likely not to destroy all your mental faculties with immediate effect). The trouble is that after a single glass, the numbers can easily become confusing. The clever counterfeiters are obviously keen drinkers.
- *Malibu* is transformed into Marabou – a poor copy with the bottle far from authentic in appearance. It is interesting how copiers often choose names which resemble how you would pronounce the world famous brand if you had drunk an entire bottle of it.
- *Baileys* is shortened to Bailes – the bottle is similar, but the product is one letter short of a cream liquer.
- *Tia Maria* appears in various guises as Zia Marina, Tia Lia and Bella Maria – while foreign sounding names appear good ideas, they offer many possibilities for the imaginative copier.
- *Johnnie Walker* is comically Johnnie Hawker, Joe Worker and Johnny Black – the traditional kind of international whiskies is more open to counterfeiting than most. It is not a practice United Distillers views lightly.

Note

1   Lieber, Ronald, "Just redo it," *Fortune*, June 23, 1997.

Red Cross

n this age of branding it is easy to overlook the branding of non-profit organizations. This, inevitably, is increasingly important as they, too, compete for our attention in a crowded marketplace. Already, outside the business arena, we see political parties perfecting their branding skills. The new political forces of the future are likely to be those which are the most adept at developing their brands and bringing their brands to our attention most successfully. Organizations such as Greenpeace and Amnesty International are already adept at maximizing the impact of their messages and of their brands.

Elsewhere, branding is increasingly important. In sports, there is the ultimate brand, the Olympics. Even maladroit administrators cannot dim the power of the Olympic brand. Companies are prepared to pay tens of millions of dollars to be associated with the brand.

The benchmark for a non-profit band, however, remains the Red Cross. Its simple logo is one of the best known in the world; its brand reputation undimmed by the passage of time. In a cynical age, the Red Cross brand remains true to its original values in a way few – if any – brands have managed. It is impartial, neutral, independent and humanitarian.

There are now 160 Red Cross national societies as well as the International Committee of the Red Cross and the International Federation of Red Cross and Red Crescent Societies. (Even the bewildering haze of bureaucracy fails to dim the power of the Red Cross brand.) The Red Cross is truly global, in a way most commercial organizations can only dream. Most countries have Red Cross societies – in Muslim countries these are called Red Crescent and in Israel Magen David Adom.

The red dawn

As with most brands, happenstance and coincidence played a part in the development of the Red Cross. In the 1850s Henry Dunant (1828–1910) ran the Swiss colony of Sétif in Algeria. He wanted to build a wheat mill but couldn't obtain the land concession required to do so. In search of a document, Dunant decided to go to the man at the top – in this case Napoleon III.

Napoleon III was, at the time, fighting another battle – this time in northern Italy. Dunant set off to find him. Along the way, Dunant happened on the Battle of Solferino in Lombardy. It was a life-changing experience. Dunant spent days working in the aftermath of the battle to tend the wounded and save lives. He later wrote *A Memory of Solferino,* in which he wrote: "Would it not be possible, in time of peace and quiet, to form relief societies for the purpose of having care given to the wounded in wartime by zealous, devoted and thoroughly qualified volunteers?"

The answer was affirmative. On 17 February 1863 the International Committee of the Red Cross met for the first time. Its work – accurately mapped out by Dunant – continues to be carried out in the former Yugoslavia, Somalia and Armenia. The American Red Cross alone gave $22 million to Rwandan refugees in Zaire.

The broader branding lessons are simple. First, identity is crucial. The Red Cross recognized at its very first meeting that is volunteers needed some mark or symbol by which they could be identified. A symbol, whether it is a red cross or a Nike swoosh, is a powerful means of identification no matter where you are or what you are doing.

Second, the great brands are closely aligned with clearly delineated values. The Red Cross's values are self-evident. Perhaps most importantly, they are continually reinforced by what is practised in the field. Red Cross volunteers simply and bravely put the organization's values into practice. The values which support the brand are continually bolstered and re-emphasized.

Third, globalization may be corporate flavor of the month, but the truly great have long practiced and preached international perspectives and awareness. Great brands break down national barriers because they do not consider them as barriers.

Reuters

euters was the first of the great information brands. The original business was based on transmitting stock market and commodity prices across a gap in the telegraph system between Belgium and Germany, but the company soon recognized the value of news reports. It created one of the most famous and respected brands in news gathering. News coming in from the Reuters wire was often the first indication newspapers had of a major story breaking.

Most people still associate the brand with the international news wire service that bears its name, but in reality the wheel has come full circle, with Reuters' main activities focused on the provision of financial data. Today, media products only account for about seven percent of the company's revenue. This is dwarfed by the revenue generated from the provision of financial data to the financial community. In particular, Reuters is the market leader in the supply of real time information via computer terminals installed in dealing rooms all around the world.

But whether the data is destined for the media or a Wall Street trader the principle is the same. In the world of information the brand is everything. The reputation of the provider is the only guarantee customers have on the quality of the data they receive.

With no time to check the reliability of the source, the brand is everything. For more than a century, Reuters has successfully combined its two core brand values: accuracy and speed. It has made the company one of the most prodigious cash generating machines on the planet.

Pigeon posts profits

In 1850, Julius Reuter set up a business to bridge the gap in the telegraph wire between Belgium and Germany. There he built a company on one simple realization: that customers would be prepared to pay for information that was timely and accurate. He used carrier pigeons to forward stock market and commodity prices from Brussels, where the Belgian telegraph line ended, to Aachen, where the German line began.

On the early receipt of critical information, fortunes could be made and lost on the stock markets, or bourses, of Europe. Those whose money was at stake had to be sure the information was accurate. They were prepared to pay handsomely for early news from a reputable source.

In 1851, he moved to London, the financial center of the Victorian world. News, Reuters grasped, was a valuable commodity. In London he launched the famous telegraph agency. By the end of the 1850s he had succeeded in establishing a standard for news gathering and distribution. Reuter set out to be "first with the news." Above speed he placed accuracy, and alongside accuracy he set impartiality of distribution. Achieving objectivity in reporting is more difficult, but is something that Reuters has earned an enviable reputation for. Today, the strength of the Reuters brand is based on the core values that its founder inculcated.

Reuter began carrying news reports of events on the mainland of Europe to leading British newspapers. Eventually, he persuaded even the *London Times* to publish his reports. This presented him with an opportunity to build his brand. For the first time, the Reuters name appeared as the source under news reports. The move marked a milestone in the branding of information.

An early scoop involved Reuters transmitting a summary of an important speech by the King of Sardinia which had important implications for the unification of Italy. His remarks were read in England the same day. The report from *The Times'* own correspondent didn't appear until four days later. (Another scoop wrongly attributed to Reuters involved a speech by Napoleon III a few days earlier; on that occasion, however, the news agency was beaten by *The Times*.)

For a century, Reuters was particularly the news agency of the British Empire. This allowed the company to grow rapidly throughout the first half of the twentieth century. As Britain's imperial power waned, Reuters moved into selling economic information to the world's trading community. This generated annual pre-tax profits of £280 million by the end of the 1980s.

The arrival of technology simply speeded up the process. In the 1970s the company was quick to make the transition from mainframe computers to desk-based PCs. The new technology allowed it to extend its brand. It also allowed it to take market share from Dow Jones its American rival.

The early 1970s saw Reuters develop a number of new technologically driven services, including a foreign exchange service, Reuters Monitor Money Rates which was introduced in 1973. The system strengthened Reuters grip on the highly lucrative market for financial data, and moved its brand onto desks on Wall Street and the City of London.

The first system was followed by others. Market dominance meant updating technology was a profitable activity. In this and other markets it benefited greatly from a combination of an established and trusted brand and, in many cases, being the first into new markets.

For a company its size, the financial performance of the business is impressive. In the 11 years to 1996, its turnover increased by a factor of six to £2.9 billion, and profits jumped from £54 million to £701 million.

The current CEO Peter Job, who joined the company as a journalist, explains the company's success simply: "If we have something good, we believe we should carpet the world with it. Over the last ten years our main challenge has been to occupy the empty hills."

As its markets became more mature, however, that began to alter. Not only were there fewer empty hills to occupy, but the competition was beginning to get there first. What really put the cat among the carrier pigeons was the arrival of some serious competition from another information provider Bloomberg's, the creation of entrepreneur Michael Bloomberg.

In recent years, Reuters has also suffered at the hands of its own customers, Some of the market analysts and brokers it supplies information to have complained that the company has underperformed. In particular, they would like to see Reuters do something exciting with the cash mountain it is sitting on. CEO Peter Job, however, is reluctant to make a big acquisition just for the sake of it – or to make news to please the stock market.

More of a threat to the long-term future of the brand is an element of arrogance that could be settling on the company's headquarters in London's Fleet Street. Recent blunders include an unsuccessful attempt to extend the Reuters brand into broadcasting.

The company has also received setbacks in Russia and Asia. But these are unlikely to cause any lasting damage. In a world that is ever hungrier for information, however, the company would have to do something spectacularly foolish to downgrade its brand. The tricky bit will be identifying new opportunities and picking the right technologies. Both are areas that Reuters has shown itself to be adept in the past.

Rolls-Royce

There has never been another brand quite like Rolls-Royce. The name itself is quite simply a by-word for the very finest quality. When Charles Rolls and Henry Royce gave their names to the famous marque they had one simple goal. The Rolls-Royce company was founded in 1904 for the purpose of building "the best car in the world."

They succeeded in spectacular fashion. Down the years, the name of their famous creation became synonymous with engineering excellence and the very finest quality. Other brands, such as Hoover and Xerox, have become interchangeable with the product they adorn. But only Rolls-Royce is used universally to describe products or services that exceed all industry standards.

Rolls Royce has a lesson for marketers everywhere. It proves that you can have the best brand in the world and still not have a viable business. In 1998, the legendary brand became the prize in a tug of war between two German car makers Volkswagen and BMW. Volkswagen won, putting $703 million in cash on the table to buy Rolls-Royce Motor Cars from British engineering group Vickers (Vickers retained the aircraft engine company). After more than 90 years, and despite the best efforts of a hurriedly formed consortium of patriotic Rolls-Royce devotees, the luxury car brand finally passed out of British hands.

In reality, the problem for Rolls was that its cars were built to such a high specification that they were uneconomic. There simply weren't enough people prepared to pay the premium prices that the traditional manufacturing processes and quality components demanded. Rolls never made it into mass production. Its annual sales of fewer than 2000 are a drop in the automobile ocean compared to other luxury car makers. By the latter part of the twentieth century it had become a luxuriously appointed anachronism: a beautiful relic from a time when motor cars were built by craftsmen for kings and queens, and cigar smoking business tycoons. Those days have passed into the mists of history.

Starter motors

The Rolls-Royce Company grew out of the electrical and mechanical engineering business established by Henry Royce in 1884. Royce built his first car in 1904, the same year that he met his future partner Charles Rolls, whose London-based company C.S. Rolls & Co. sold luxury cars. The two men struck a deal, that Royce should manufacture a new range of cars to be sold exclusively by C.S. Rolls & Co. and which would bear both of their names.

The success of the venture led to the formation of the Rolls-Royce Company in 1906, and to the launch of the Silver Ghost. Within the year, it was hailed by the British press as the "best car in the world." The rest of the world, however, would require some more convincing. In time, though, it too became captivated by the brand.

In response to the threat of war, Henry Royce then designed his first aircraft engine – dubbed the Eagle. The engine powered half the allied aircraft in the air war. The company went on to design the engines that powered the Hawker Hurricane and Supermarine Spitfire which played a decisive role in the Battle of Britain.

In 1966, the car and aircraft engine company merged with Bristol Siddeley, the other major British manufacturer of aero engines, consolidating the British industry. But it was the Rolls-Royce car that enshrined the romance of the brand. Successive models rolled off the assembly line to become almost instant classics. The Silver Shadow followed in the majestic tire tracks and tradition of the Silver Ghost.

For the rich and famous, R&R (rest and relaxation) in an RR was the perfect combination. Its unique aura gave rise to names that could only be bestowed on the most noble of automobiles adorned with the famous Rolls-Royce insignia. Romantic they were, practical they were not. The Rolls-Royce could never be an economy car. A smaller engine, or plastic dashboard, just wasn't an option.

In its love affair with the impractical, the British motor car industry is probably unsurpassed. Other famous marques have suffered a similar fate. Popularized by James Bond, Aston Martin never once made a profit in its entire history under British ownership, and was eventually acquired by Ford. Jaguar also succumbed, while others simply disappeared from the road to be glimpsed only in museums and the garages of collectors.

But Rolls-Royce was special. More special even than Aston. In a world dominated by disposable products, it stood for something nobler than simply making money. To some, Rolls-Royce stood for a finer aspiration. A dream of perfection: with the famous Spirit of Ecstasy gracing its radiator. To others, it was little more than a symbol of the end of the British empire, and its passing into German hands merely a confirmation of where the future of Europe's quality car industry really lies.

There is rich irony in the fact that Rolls-Royce, once the car maker of choice for royal families, now belongs to Volkswagen, which started life as the "people's car." VW endeared itself to millions by producing an ugly duckling of a car called the Beetle. Its most important characteristic was its cheeky but basic utilitarianism. Few brands could start life so far apart.

By snatching Roll-Royce from under the very nose of its more aristocratic suitor BMW, VW acquired one of the superbrands of the quality car market.

According to one German auto analyst, the match is not as unsuitable as it might at first appear. "Practically overnight Volkswagen has acquired the luxury image it longed for." VW still has formally to secure the right to use the famous logo and trademark held by the Rolls-Royce company which makes aircraft engines. On the side of the flying angel, the arrival of VW should bring much needed investment to revitalize production and restore it Rolls-Royce to its former glory.

The deal was just one of the seismic upheavals among automobile manufacturers and the European car industry in particular. In recent years, Ford has acquired Jaguar and a sizeable share in Mazda, while General Motors now owns half of the Swedish car maker Saab. BMW bought Rover, and most spectacular of all, in 1998 Chrysler merged with Daimler-Benz.

What surprised some industry insiders was that the powers that be at BMW allowed the brand to slip through its fingers. In Rover, BMW had already bought the rest of the British car industry, so why let the jewel in the crown go to another? The company, which supplies the engines to some Rolls-Royce models, refused to increase its original bid. If Rolls was sold to another company, it warned that the supply of engines might stall. To neutralize the threat, VW made a bid for Cosworth, a leading British engine maker. In the end, money – in the form of a bigger bid from Volkswagen – won the day. At the last, the British management took a practical view of their most impractical asset.

If the story has a moral it is simply that real superbrands do not die, they simply pass to the highest bidder.

Sears, Roebuck

T here was a time when markets lay undiscovered and untapped; huge vistas lay waiting to be discovered. Those lucky enough to do so often changed the shape of entire industries. Sears, Roebuck is one such story. The Sears story is basically one of the discovery of a vast new market: the rural, isolated, farming community of the USA.

In the 1880s, the total population of the USA was 58 million, around a sixth of its current population. The majority of people lived in the countryside – around 65 percent. Richard Sears was one of them. He lived in the isolated outpost of North Redwood, Minnesota where he was an agent of the Minneapolis and St Louis railway station. Trains didn't stop often in North Redwood, so Sears traded a few things when they came his way – things like lumber and coal. One of the items that came Sears' way was a consignment of watches. These sold well so Sears ordered some more and, in 1886, started the RW Sears Watch Company in Minneapolis.

Sears then moved to Chicago and recruited Alvah C. Roebuck to help him. In 1893 Sears, Roebuck & Company was born. The company moved into the mail order business selling watches and jewelry. By 1895 the catalog was 532 pages long and included everything from fishing tackle to glassware; millinery to saddles. In 1893 sales were $400,000; in 1895, they were over $750,000.

At this point the company was a huge success. But the challenge was to take it further. In 1895, a Chicago clothing manufacturer called Julius Rosenwald bought a share in the company. It was Rosenwald who built on the lucrative foundations established by the entrepreneurial Sears and Roebuck.

The detail of retail

"Richard Sears gave the company his name. But it was not he who made it into a modern business enterprise," Peter Drucker recounts in *The Practice of Management.* "Sears's own operations could hardly be called a 'business.' He was a shrewd speculator, buying up distress-merchandise and offering it, one batch at a time, through spectacular advertising. Every one of his deals was a complete transaction in itself which, when finished, liquidated itself and the business with it. But his way of operation could never found a business, let alone perpetuate it. In fact, he would have been forced out of business within a few years, as all the many people before him had been who operated on a similar basis."

This is probably a little harsh on Sears, who brought entrepreneurial energy to the company. One of his initiatives, for example, was a system of rewards for customers who passed copies of the catalog onto friends and relatives. This was tested out in Iowa. Customers received 24 copies of the catalog to distribute. If the recipients of the catalogs placed an order, the original customers received rewards.

However, Julius Rosenwald brought business vigor to the company. In 1906 Sears, Roebuck opened its Chicago mail-order plant. It was the largest business building in the world with three million square feet of floor space. Size, however, was not necessarily equated with efficiency. The Sears business was sprawling and inefficient. Customers sometimes received five articles when they wanted one or simply none at all. The logistics were a nightmare.

The company got its act together. A time schedule was introduced so that once orders were received they were given a time to be dispatched. An array of belts and chutes linked arrivals and departures. Henry Ford was reputedly to have been inspired to introduce his mass production methods after seeing them at work in the Sears, Roebuck warehouse.

The next challenge for the company was to deal with growing competition from retail chains. This was hitting Sears' catalog sales. Also, the move from the country to the city was now underway – by

1920 America's urban population outnumbered its rural population for the first time. Clearly, this had a substantial effect on Sears' core market.

After failing to convince Montgomery Ward to move into retailing, Robert E. Wood (1879–1969) was hired by Sears Roebuck in 1924. Julius Rosenwald liked the idea of moving into retail stores; Sears opened its first retail store in 1925 and became the world's largest general merchandiser. By 1928 Sears had 192 retail stores. A heady pace of expansion was maintained – during a single year in he 1920s a new Sears store opened every other business day. By 1931, the retail stores formed the bulk of the company's business.

The rest of the company's history has been less distinguished. Empires disappear as surely in commerce as they do elsewhere. Even so, Sears remains a formidable retail force with 833 department stores, over 1,300 other stores, and an array of products sold through independently owned stores.

The Sears story

- 1886: Richard Sears starts selling watches to supplement his income.
- 1887: Sears moves to Chicago and recruits Alvah Roebuck.
- 1888: First catalog produced.
- 1893: Sears, Roebuck & Company founded.
- 1896: First large-scale catalog.
- 1911: Sets up testing lab.
- 1925: First retail store.
- 1945: Sales exceed $1 billion.
- 1973: Moves HQ to Chicago's Sears Tower.
- 1981: Acquires Dean Witter Reynolds and Coldwell, Banker & Co.

D uring the 1970s, Japanese giant Matsushita developed VHS video and made the decision to license the technology. Sony developed the immeasurably better Betamax but failed to license it. The world standard is VHS and Betamax is consigned to history. This is probably the only missed opportunity in the short but hugely successful history of Sony, the company that first conquered Japan and then the world.

Akito Morita (born 1921) was an officer in the Japanese Navy during World War II. Trained as a physicist and scientist, Morita could have followed family tradition and gone into sake production. (He refers to himself as "the first son and fifteenth generation heir to one of Japan's finest and oldest sake-brewing families.") Instead, he founded a company with Masaru Ibuka (1908–97) immediately after the end of the war.

The duo invested the equivalent of £845 and set themselves up in business in a bombed-out Tokyo department store. Ibuka was the technical expert; Morita the salesman. The company, was christened Tokyo Tsushin Kogyo KK (Tokyo Telecommunications Engineering Corporation). Not a good name to put on a product, Morita later ruminated. Initially, the company made radio parts and a rice cooker, among other things. Its rice cooker was unreliable. Today, Ibuka and Morita's organization is a $45 billion company with over 100,000 employees. According to one Harris poll, the company is America's most respected brand.

The innovation express

In 1949 the company developed magnetic recording tape and, in 1950, sold the first tape recorder in Japan. In 1957 the company produced a pocket sized radio and a year later renamed itself Sony (*sonus* is Latin for sound). The Sony name remains prominent on all of its products. In 1960 Sony produced the first transistor TV in the world. And increasingly the world was Sony's market. Its combination of smaller and smaller products at the leading edge of technology proved irresistible.

In 1961 Sony Corporation of American was the first Japanese company to be listed on Wall Street and, in 1989, Sony bought Columbia Pictures so that by 1991 it had more foreigners on its 135,000 payroll than Japanese. Morita became famous as the acceptable face of Japanese industry. Sophisticated and entrepreneurial, he did not fit the Western stereotype. (He also advocated a more assertive Japanese approach in *The Japan That Can Say No* which he wrote with a Japanese politician, Ishihara Shintaro.)

In 1993 Morita resigned as Sony chairman after suffering a cerebral hemorrhage playing tennis. In the same year, the company wrote off $3.2 billion for its movie operations – the major misadventure in its history. Even so, the modern Sony is a $37 billion company.

Morita and Sony's story parallels the rebirth of Japan as an industrial power. "We in the free world can do great things. We proved it in Japan by changing the image of Made in Japan from something shoddy to something fine," says Morita. When Sony was first attempting to make inroads into Western markets it cannot be forgotten that Japanese products were sneered at as being of the lowest quality. Surmounting that obstacle was a substantial business achievement.

Morita and Sony's gift was to invent new markets. Describing what he called Sony's "pioneer spirit," Morita said: "Sony is a pioneer and never intends to follow others. Through progress, Sony wants to serve the whole world. It shall be always a seeker of the unknown … Sony has a principle of respecting and encouraging one's ability and always tries to bring out the best in a person. This is the vital force of Sony." While companies such as Matsushita were inspired followers, Sony set a cracking pace with product after product, innovation after innovation.

Sony brought the world the hand-held video camera, the first home video recorder and the floppy disc. Its most famous success was the brainchild of Morita, the Walkman. The evolution of this now ubiquitous product is the stuff of corporate legend. Morita noticed that young people liked listening to music wherever they went. He put two and two together and made a Walkman. "I do not believe that any amount of market research could have told us that it would have been successful," he said adding the rider – "The public does not know what is possible, we do."

Such brilliant marketing was no mere accident. "If you go through life convinced that your way is always best, all the new ideas in the world will pass you by," says Morita who argues that analysis and education do not necessarily get you to the best business decisions. "You can be totally rational with a machine. But if you work with people, sometimes logic often has to take a backseat to understanding," he says. Morita is also the author of *Never Mind School Records*.

Apart from his marketing prowess, Morita has emphasized the cultural differences in Japanese attitudes towards work. "Never break another man's rice bowl," he advises and observes: "Japanese people tend to be much better adjusted to the notion of work, any kind of work, as honorable." Management is regarded by Morita as where the buck stops and starts: "If we face a recession, we should not lay off employees; the company should sacrifice a profit. It's management's risk and management's responsibility. Employees are not guilty; why should they suffer?"

Morita's legacy of responsible management backed by imaginative marketing continues. Echoing the company creator's philosophy, the current president of Sony Corp, Nobuyuki Idei, says: "Right now, you don't need to be an engineer. You have to have a nose, and if you don't you can't run a company like Sony."[1]

Sony and so far

- 1946: Masaru Ibuka and Akito Morita invested £845 to start their company.
- 1954: Tokyo Tsuchin Kogyo licenced to make transistors. It makes Japan's first transistor and the first all-transistor radio.
- 1968: First Trinitron color TV.
- 1971: First color video cassette.
- 1975: Betamax VCR – first home use video system.
- 1979: The Sony Walkman.
- 1981: Sony electrical camera.
- 1982: World's first CD player.
- 1983: First consumer camcorder.
- 1985: First digital VTR.
- 1988: Sony bought CBS Records to form Sony Music Entertainment.
- 1989: Acquires Columbia Pictures to form Sony Pictures Entertainment; Sony launches 3.5 inch micro floppy disk.
- 1995: Play Station launched.
- 1999: Launch of Pocket Station.

Note

1   Gibney, Frank, "A new world at Sony," *Time*, November 17, 1997.

I n 1971 Gerald Baldwin, Gordon Bowker and Zev Siegl opened a gourmet coffee store in Seattle's Pike Place Market. To launch the business they raised $10,000. The trio called their enterprise Starbucks. (Their belief was that the "St" sound was memorable and alluring.)

The coffee store – pointedly not a "coffee shop" – started as it meant to go by making money. Within a year Starbucks was in profit and, in 1973, began roasting its own coffee. Starbucks evolved and, in 1982, brought in Howard Schultz to help with its marketing. Schultz had grown up in Brooklyn and went to college on a football scholarship at North Michigan University. He later became a Xerox salesman.

In 1983 Starbucks acquired Peet's and co-founder Gerald Baldwin eventually left to run Peet's. Then the revolution began. In 1987 Howard Schultz bought out the Starbucks management team for $4 million. (Business trivia: Bill Gates Sr helped Schultz draw up his bid.) Schultz remains the company's chairman and CEO.

Building from granules

Schultz broadened the company's horizons. He opened a store in Chicago. It took off. More followed. And then more. The approach was a branding classic. "The goal was to add value to a commodity typically purchased on supermarket aisles," said Schultz. "Our so-called baristas [bartenders] introduce customers to the fine coffees of the world the way wine stewards bring forward fine wines."[1]

Starbucks offered excellent service combined with a rejuvenated product. "Starbucks is not a trend. We're a lifestyle," he proclaimed with all due flakiness. The Starbucks training manual explains how it breathed latte into what was once pond water: "As Americans, we have grown up thinking of coffee primarily as a hot, tan liquid dispensed from fairly automatic appliances, then 'doctored' as needed to make it drinkable ... The opposite of this approach is to treat coffee making as a brand of cooking. You start with the best beans you can buy, making sure they are fresh. You use your favorite recipe. You grind the beans to the right consistency and add delicious, fresh-tasting water."

It did little advertising to build its brand strength. "We concentrated on creating value and customer service," says Schultz. "Our success proves you can build a national brand without 30 second sound bites."[2] Between 1987 and 1998 Starbucks spent less than $10 million on advertising.

Its emphasis instead has been on building a network of alliances that make its products more widely available. It has, for example, established alliances with Barnes & Noble, Costco, Horizon and United Airlines. (The lure can be understood by the fact that the tie up with United exposes 75 million travelers to Starbucks products.) Starbucks has also worked on a wide variety of spin-offs. There is Starbucks ice-cream with Dreyer's Grand; bottled Frapuccino developed with Pepsi; and even a (nightmarish) coffee-laced beer with the Redhook Ale Company.

This, of course, runs the risk of getting into bed with the wrong partner. Schultz is confident that this can be avoided: "I don't think we are cannibalizing ourselves as long as we continue to introduce and offer best-of-class products."

Starbucks' approach has been compared to that of Wal-Mart. This is not something the company takes too kindly to. The suggestion is that it has muscled in, using its rapidly increasing size to squeeze smaller competitors into the cold. This rests uneasily with the ambience that Starbucks has carefully assembled around its band. It talks of "elevating the coffee experience" and is keen on new age philosophizing.

Along the way, Schultz – the "espresso evangelist" according to one newspaper – has developed a humanitarian management style. "What we've done is we've said the most important component in our brand is the employee," says Schultz. "The people have created the magic. The people have created the experience." His autobiography is suitably entitled *Pour Your Heart Into It*.

In 1992 the company went public. Its stock doubled in value in five months. (Schultz's stake was worth $70 million.) The company's mermaid logo is now omnipresent. Starbucks has 1600 coffee shops in the US and turnover of $1.3 billion. It aims for 2000 stores by 2000. It now eyes the world with latte eyes. Starbucks opened in London in 1998 and plans 500 European shops by 2003. When its store opened in Tokyo, hundreds queued.

Notes

1   Ioannon, Lori, "Making customers come back for more," *Fortune*, March 16, 1998.
2   Ioannon, Lori, "Making customers come back for more," *Fortune*, March 16, 1998.

Swatch

In 1979 Ernest Thomke developed the Swatch watch. Almost overnight the dormant Swiss watch industry was revived. The humble timepiece became a fashion accessory and Swiss market share of the watch industry rose from 15 percent to over 50 percent.

Swatch was a brand born out of the crisis affecting Swiss watch making. When the brightly colored watches made their first appearance in 1983, they seemed to be the antithesis of everything Swiss watch making stood for. It is a classic example of a brand that defied received wisdom to change the rules of its industry.

An earlier attempt to launch the new product in America in 1982 was a dismal failure. It was only when the product was advertised as the "second watch" under the slogan: You have a second home, why not a second watch?" that it became a hit with consumers. This was shortened to the "s" watch, which became the Swatch brand we know today.

The first Swatches had fewer than 51 parts, far less than any other analog quartz watch. A traditional mechanical watch, by contrast, had more than 125 parts. The people behind the upstart watches gambled that consumers couldn't care less about the number of parts, but would find novelty in the profusion of Swatch styles. The gamble paid off. A new brand in watches had arrived.

The Swatch was made not by Swiss craftsmen but by robots. Manufacturing costs were low. Swatches were sealed into plastic cases. Repair was not an option. Unlike earlier Swiss watches it was not meant to be handed down from father to son, rather it was the ultimate in disposable time pieces. Consumers were invited to throw away their old Swatch and buy another. Key to the brand positioning was the fresh appeal of a constant supply of new designs. For the first time, watches changed with the season.

In an industry characterized by conservative values, the Swatch was different, cool and fun. The secret to keeping the brand strong lay with constant innovation. New designs and colors, changing every six months at first and then more frequently, assured return buyers. Keen pricing, they sold for between $25 and $35, assured they were affordable for young people. By 1997, more than 200 million units had been sold.

Calling time on the old watch industry

The Swatch story is a classic tale of triumph over adversary. Between the mid-1970s and 1983, the Swiss watch making industry saw its share of the world watch market decimated from 30 percent to just 9 percent, a loss of two-thirds in under ten years. As Japanese watches swept all before them, the Swiss were losing out even in their traditional stronghold in quality time pieces. The writing was on the wall for what was once regarded as the finest watchmakers in the world.

It seemed that only a miracle could save the Swiss watch industry from closures. A miracle is what they got: a branding miracle called Swatch.

An attempt to rescue the ailing watch industry was made through the formation of a consortium of leading Swiss manufacturers. It included some of the best-known Swiss watch brands. The consortium called ASUAG-SSIH, was later reformed with the help of businessman Nicolas Hayek as SMH – the Swiss Corporation for Microelectronics and Watchmaking Industries, and ultimately became the Swatch Group.

But it was Ernst Thomke, president of ETA SA and ETA's chief engineer Jacques Muller who came up with the winning idea. Thomke had developed the Delirium, then the slimmest watch in the world. He suggested a low-cost version of the Delirium to combat the Japanese threat. It was Thomke who developed technical specification of the original Swatch, as well as the all-important marketing concept.

The creation of the first Swatch was fraught with problems. For one thing, Thomke had secretly to buy the patent rights to manufacture key components of his daring creation. The traditional manufacturing facilities in Switzerland were forbidden to produce coils or work with plastics.

Research and development was carried out in secret. Nicolas Hayek, acting as adviser to the watch industry, supported the project and played a key role in making sure that production stayed in Switzerland.

Hayek became chairman and CEO of the Swatch Group in 1986, after it was created out of the merger of the ASUAG and SSIH watch companies. The Group, which also markets the brands Blancpain, Omega, Longines, Rado, Tissot, Certina, Mido, Hamilton, Balmain, Calvin Klein, Flik Flak and Lanco, has its headquarters in Biel-Bienne.

Hayek is credited with implementing the plan put forward by Thomke, and with reviving the Swiss watch industry.

Changing times

The pace with which new designs and new technology is introduced has always been key to keeping the Swatch brand fresh. In recent years, for example, new developments have taken place alongside the standard plastic Swatch. New models have been introduced including the Chrono and the Irony (a metal watch, which provides the ironic twist to the Swatch concept).

Other novelty innovations include the light-powered Swatch Solar; the melodic alarm of the Swatch MusiCall; the world's first watch with a built-in pager called the Beep Swatch. Another typical Swatch innovation is the Access, with built-in access control function which can be used as a ski pass at many of the world's ski resorts.

Such timely departures have helped keep the Swatch in the number one position in the world watch industry. In 1997, Swatch achieved a turnover of over 3000 million Swiss Francs. Not bad for a brand that's still in its teens.

Toyota

In 1918 Sakichi Toyoda formed a company called the Toyoda Spinning & Weaving Co. In the 1930s the development of automatic looms convinced the company that its future lay elsewhere. Kiichiro Toyoda, the founder's son, had studied engineering and visited the US and Europe. He decided the future lay in car making and changed the company's name to Toyota in 1936. (The name Toyota emerged from a competition – Toyota in Japanese characters conveys speed and uses eight strokes, a number suggesting prosperity. From the Western perspective it is pronounceable and attractively meaningless.) Kiichiro Toyoda remained as company president until 1950 and the company was run by a member of the Toyoda family until 1995.

The first Toyota car was the Model AA. (As something of an insurance policy, the company also continued in its old business – looms were still produced until the early 1950s.) In the 1950s Toyota established offices in Taiwan and Saudi Arabia. It began making forklift trucks (and is now the world number one in that market) and entered the American market (1958) and later the UK market (1965).

Its initial foray into the US proved unsuccessful. Its Crown model was designed for the Japanese market and was ill-suited to American freeways. Eventually Toyota got it right. In 1968 the success of the Corolla enabled it to make a great leap forwards – by 1975 it had replaced Volkswagen as the US's number one auto importer. It got right in the heart of the American market in 1984 when Toyota entered into a joint venture with General Motors to build Toyotas in the US. (The joint venture also makes the GM Prizm.) Along the way, Toyota established an unrivaled reputation for build quality. The brand became synonymous with reliability – no bad thing for a car company.

More successes have followed. The Camry was the best selling car in the US in 1997. Toyota is now developing its interests in "hybrid-electric" cars – launched in Japan in 1997, they are being

202 • The Ultimate Book of Brands

rolled out globally in 2000. It is also involved in financial services, telecommunications and housing, marine engines and recreational boats, parts distribution and aviation services.

Lean means Toyota

Toyota is now the third biggest car maker in the world (behind GM and Ford). It sells five million vehicles a year (1.3 million in North America, 2 million in Japan and 0.5 million in Europe). In Japan it has nearly 40 percent of the market. Its 1998 sales were $88.5 billion with a net income of $3.5 billion.

Central to this huge success is the simple fact that in terms of production, Toyota has constantly remained a step ahead of its Western competitors. The reason for this can be seen if you go into the Toyota headquarters building. There you will find three portraits. One is of the company's founder; the next of the company's current president; and the final one is a portrait of the American quality guru, W. Edwards Deming. While Western companies produced gas-guzzling cars with costly, large and unhappy workforces in the 1970s, Toyota was forging ahead with implementation of Deming's ideas. In the early 1980s, Western companies finally woke up and began to implement Deming's quality gospel. By then it was too late. Toyota had moved on. (In fact, it didn't mind telling Western companies all about total quality management for this very reason.)

Toyota progressed to what became labeled lean production, or the Toyota Production System. (The architect of this is usually acknowledged as being Taichi Ohno who wrote a short book on the Toyota approach and later became a consultant.) From Toyota's point of view, there was nothing revolutionary in lean production. In fact, lean production was an integral part of Toyota's commitment to quality and its roots can be traced back to the 1950s. It was only in 1984, when Toyota opened up its joint venture with General Motors in California, that the West began to wake up and the word began to spread.

And the word was based on three simple principles. The first was that of just-in-time production. There is no point in producing cars, or anything else, in blind anticipation of someone buying them. Waste ("muda") is bad. Production has to be closely tied to the market's requirements. Second, responsibility for quality rests with everyone and any quality defects need to be rectified as soon as they are identified. The third, more elusive, concept was the "value stream." Instead of seeing the company as a series of unrelated products and processes, it should be seen as a continuous and uniform whole, a stream including suppliers as well as customers.

The Lexus conquers all

Toyota's production philosophy and the carefully developed strength of its brand reached its high point in 1990 with the launch of the Lexus. The Lexus was initially greeted as a triumph for Japanese imitation. Media pundits laughed at the company's effrontery – "If Toyota could have slapped a Mercedes star on the front of the Lexus, it would have fooled most of the people most of the time."

With the Lexus, Toyota moved the goalposts. It out-engineered Mercedes and BMW. (Toyota is keen to tell you that the Lexus took seven years; $2 billion; 1400 engineers; 2300 technicians; 450 prototypes; and generated 200 patents.) Its standard fittings include a satellite navigation system and much more. Toyota made great play of the fact that the car was tested in Japan on mile after mile of carefully built highways that exactly imitated roads in the US, Germany or the UK. Toyota even put in the right road signs.

While the product stood up to scrutiny, where Lexus really stole a march on its rivals was through the Lexus ownership experience. Even when things went wrong, the service was good. An early problem led to a product recall. Lexus had dealers call up people personally and immediately. Instead of having a negative effect it strengthened the brand. Lexus screwed things up like everyone else, but then they sorted the problem out in a friendly, human way. With the Lexus, Toyota proved that its capacity to stay ahead of the pack remains undiminished.

*V*irgin

"I believe there is almost no limit to what a brand can do, but only if used properly," says Richard Branson, founder of the Virgin empire. In the past two decades, Richard Branson has rewritten the rules of branding.

Branson's greatest achievement, to date, is to create what is arguably the world's first universal brand. Other famous names have become synonymous with the product they adorn: Hoover vacuum cleaners, Coca-Cola, and Levi Strauss to name just a few. But Virgin is alone among Western brands in its ability to transcend products. Never before has a single brand been so successfully deployed across such a diverse range of goods and services. It has been used to sell everything from vodka to financial services, bridal gowns to the Sex Pistols.

The most important aspect of the Virgin brand proposition is its credibility among its market segment. There is a potential downside. Just as existing Virgin products and services provide credibility for new offerings, the relationship between the Virgin family could also work in reverse. If the image were to become tarnished by association with a shoddy product or poor service or an offering that was a rip-off, then the standing of the wider Virgin brand could be damaged. The company's less than dazzling move into rail services has tested the brand to its limits. To date, its successes have far outweighed its failures.

Yet despite its remarkable success, Branson would have us believe that none of it was planned. He gives the impression that the Virgin phenomenon is one of those odd things that happen to people sometimes. This is part of the Branson mystique. He makes it look and sound so simple.

"When we came up with the name 'Virgin' instead of 'Slipped Disc' Records for our record company in the winter of 1969, I had some vague idea of the name being catchy and applying to lots of other products for young people."[1]

"It would have been interesting to have tracked the success of the Virgin companies or otherwise if we had called the company Slipped Disc Records. Slipped Disc Condoms might not have worked as well."

The quip is typical of a man who has lived his whole life like some big adventure. An outspoken critic of business schools and management theory, Branson likes to portray himself as the ordinary man on the street (despite his comfortable middle class origins). He is the small guy who outsmarts the big guys. His account of how the famous Virgin logo came to be is typical of the way things seem to happen at Virgin.

"When Virgin Records became successful we followed our instincts ...," Branson explains. "Initially the music reflected the 'hippy' era and our logo of a naked lady back to back reflected that too. Then when Punk came along we felt we needed a crisper image ... Rather than spending a fortune coming up with the new image, I was talking to our graphic designer one day explaining what we wanted and he threw on the floor his doodling – the now famous Virgin signature – which I fortunately picked up on the way to the loo."

It sounds so casual, but the words mask an extraordinary entrepreneurial mind, one that has re-invented business to fit the times he lives in. Today, Branson is the driving force at the center of a web of somewhere between 150 and 200 companies, employing more than 8000 people in 26 countries. His commercial interests span travel, hotels, consumer goods, computer games, music and airlines You can even buy a Virgin pension or investment plan.

Financial services is a far cry from the adolescent record label that helped put Punk on the map in the 1980s, with a controversially named album by the Sex Pistols. By then, Virgin had already won the respect of the hippy generation with *Tubular Bells*, from a young unknown artist called Mike Oldfield. *Never Mind the Bollocks* was the perfect product to establish the Virgin brand with a new generation of spiky haired teenagers. Branson had created a new fusion of rebellion and business – and discovered a unique new brand proposition. He has been repeating the formula ever since.

Originally aimed at younger people, as Branson has matured so too has the Virgin appeal. "Four years ago we crossed over into appealing to their parents," he says. "Now we're moving into pensions and life insurance. We haven't quite reached funeral parlours. But we have to be careful we don't lose the kids. I'd like people to feel most of their needs in life can be filled by Virgin. The absolutely critical thing is we must never let them down."[2] By the mid-1990s, the Virgin name seemed to be everywhere. So ubiquitous had the Virgin brand become that hardly a day seemed to go by without seeing a grinning Richard Branson launching some new Virgin product or service. The famous flying V logo was emblazoned on aircraft, megastore and cinema fronts, and was about to make its debut on cola cans.

The activity prompted some to question whether the Virgin brand was being diluted. Those who understood what he was about, however, recognized that what Branson had created was an entirely new kind of brand proposition. John Murphy, chairman of the famous brand consultancy Interbrand, for example, observed that: "Unless they poison someone or start applying the brand to inappropriate products such as pension funds or photocopiers, I doubt whether the Virgin brand will ever be diluted." Little did Murphy know that by 1996, Virgin Direct would be offering financial services – including pensions.

Branson has acknowledged time and time again that the most vital asset Virgin has is the reputation of its brand. Put the Virgin name on any product that doesn't come up to scratch and the whole company is brought into disrepute. "Our customers trust us," he says simply.

The Branson philosophy, then, is: look after your brand and it will last. There is, however, and always has been a tension at the heart of the Virgin brand. For all his unquestioned emphasis on the integrity of the Virgin name, one of Branson's personal characteristics – that has become a strand of what Virgin stands for – is a certain restlessness. He has an insatiable desire to take risks and explore new areas. It is in his blood that Branson has to be constantly expanding the borders of the empire. Yet it is vital to do so without damaging the good name of the company. This creates something of a dilemma. It is one that Branson is well aware of.

"We are expanding and growing our use of the brand," he says, "but are always mindful of the fact that we should only put it on products and services that fit – or will fit – our very exacting criteria."

In recent years, he has thought long and hard about what the Virgin brand stands for. He believes the reputation the company has built up is based on five key factors: value for money, quality, reliability, innovation and an indefinable, but nonetheless palpable, sense of fun. (Another, slightly snappier, version of the Virgin brand values is: genuine and fun, contemporary and different, consumers' champion, and first class at business-class price.[3])

In a classic piece of reverse engineering, these are now the brand values that Virgin applies when considering new business ventures. Any new product or service must have, or have the prospect of becoming in the future:

- the best quality;
- it must be innovative;
- it must be good value for money;
- it must be challenging to existing alternatives; and
- it must add a sense of fun or cheekiness.

Virgin claims that nine out ten projects it considers are potentially very profitable, but, if they don't fit with the Group's values, they are rejected.[4] But, says Branson, "If an idea satisfies at least four of these five criteria, we'll usually take a serious look at it."

The selling of Richard

Along the way, Branson has also successfully sold himself to millions of admiring consumers. In fact, persuading consumers to trust the company's chairman is a vital element of the Virgin brand proposition.

He may not look like a finely tuned PR machine, but Richard Branson has turned himself into a walking, talking logo. Where McDonald's has the red haired clown Ronald McDonald, and Disney has a six foot mouse; Virgin has its goofy chairman. Every time his picture appears in a newspaper or magazine, it promotes the Virgin brand.

This is entirely deliberate, and probably one of the most effective promotional strategies ever employed by a company. The risk to the reputation of the brand, of course, is correspondingly high should Branson's personal image become tarnished. To date, however, it has proved highly successful, enabling him to build the Virgin brand on a shoestring advertising budget.[5]

Calculating the advertising value of Branson's failed attempt to circumnavigate the globe in a hot air balloon in terms of column inches in newspapers and minutes on worldwide broadcast news, one American advertising executive said "there aren't enough zeros to do the maths."

With the launch of Virgin Atlantic Airways he learned a new trick. The big airlines spend literally $millions on advertising every year. Branson soon realized that free media coverage was the only way he could hope to survive. This gave rise to a series of daredevil escapades and publicity stunts. Apparently, the decision to challenge for the Blue Riband – attempting to break the record for the fastest Atlantic crossing – was made when Branson discovered he couldn't afford New York TV advertising rates to promote his airline. It is a tactic that Branson has used to remarkable effect ever since, setting aside about a quarter of his time for PR activities.[6]

His derring-do outside of business life is matched by the boldness of his escapades in it. He has repeatedly used the Virgin brand to take on aggressive market leaders and shake up complacent markets – first the big record companies, then the airlines and more recently soft drinks and financial services. These commercial adventures have almost bankrupted the company on several occasions.

But they have earned him a special place in the affections of first the British public and now the world.

But his popular image belies another side to Branson.[7] Despite his wealth, he remains unrelenting in his commercial ambitions. "A ruthlessly ambitious workaholic," is how one biographer described him.

Stretching a point

One of the most frequently asked questions about Virgin is how far the brand can stretch.

Branson's answer is that as long as the brand's integrity is not compromised, then it is infinitely elastic.

Just how powerful the Virgin brand is is shown by a recent survey. It found that 96 percent of British consumers have heard of Virgin and 96 percent can correctly name Richard Branson as its founder.

"Virgin is a unique phenomenon on the British business scene," notes one commentator. "It has, essentially, one principal asset, and an intangible one at that – its name. From financial services through airlines and railways to entertainment megastores and soft drinks, clothes and even bridal salons, the brand is instantly recognizable to the consumer, conjuring up an image of good quality, cheap prices, and a trendy hipness that few others can match."[8]

Branson intends to keep it that way. But he acknowledges that the Virgin strategy would not work for any brand; it is based on what he calls "reputational branding" rather than traditional product and service branding.

Branson's brand

- 1968: First issue of Student Magazine, Richard Branson's first business venture is produced.
- 1969: The name Virgin is chosen for the record company.
- 1970: Start of Virgin mail-order operation.
- 1971: First Virgin record store opens in London's Oxford Street.
- 1973: Virgin Record label launched with "Tubular Bells."
- 1977: Virgin signs the Sex Pistols.
- 1980: Virgin Records moves into overseas markets.
- 1983: Virgin Vision (forerunner of Virgin Communications) formed to distribute films and videos Virgin Games (computer games software publisher) is launched.
- 1984: Virgin Atlantic Airways and Virgin Cargo launched.
- 1986: Virgin Group is floated on the London Stock Exchange.
- 1987: Virgin Records America is launched, quickly followed by subsidiary in Japan. Stock market crashes, Virgin share price falls back to below 90p. Branson forced to abandon attempt at hostile takeover of EMI.
- 1988: Richard Branson announces management buy-out of Virgin Group.
- 1991: Virgin operates first Heathrow services. Branson sells 50 % of Megastores business to W. H. Smith.
- 1992: Sale of Virgin Music Group to THORN EMI.
- 1993: British Airways settles libel action for £610, 000 plus all legal costs (total costs believed to exceed £4.5 million). Virgin Radio 1215 AM launched.
- 1995: Virgin Direct Personal Financial Service is launched.
- 1996: Virgin Bride; Virgin Net; and Virgin Rail Group.
- 1997: Virgin Direct launches its first banking product, Virgin One Account.

Notes

1 Branson, Richard, BBC *Money Programme* Lecture, 1998.
2 Rodgers, Paul, "The Branson Phenomenon," *Enterprise* magazine, March–April 1997.
3 Andrew Campbell & David Sadtler, "Corporate breakups," *Strategy & Business*, Third Quarter, 1998.
4 Virgin Group literature.
5 And despite an allegation of sexual harassment.
6 Mitchell, Alan, *Leadership by Richard Branson*, Amrop International, 1995.
7 Jackson, Tim, *Virgin King*, HarperCollins, London, 1994.
8 Rodgers, Paul, "The Branson Phenomenon," *Enterprise* magazine, March–April 1997.

W al-Mart grew from a very small business to an extremely large one through the sheer force of personality and retailing insight of Sam Walton. "I have concentrated all along on building the finest retailing company that we possibly could. Period. Creating a huge personal fortune was never particularly a goal of mine," Walton reflected.[1]

Wal-Mart first came to life in 1945 in Newport, Arkansas. Aged 27, Sam Walton acquired a franchise licence for a five-and-dime store. His first year was good. Sales totalled $80,000. By the third year, the store was generating sales of $225,000. Then, in 1950, the lease came to an end. Walton moved to Bentonville, Arkansas and opened "Walton's." Soon after he added another store and, in 1962, opened his first large scale rural discount store.

Today Wal-Mart is bigger than Sears, K-Mart and JC Penney combined with annual sales of $117,958 million. The company serves over 90 million people every week. There are 1879 Wal-Mart stores, 512 Supercenters and 446 Sam's Clubs. Wal-Mart also operates in Canada, Germany, Mexico, Puerto Rico and Brazil, as well as having joint ventures in China and Korea. There are 780,000 Wal-Mart associates in the US alone and a further 115,000 across the world. The Walton family still own around 38 percent of this colossus.

Business the Walton way

Walton succeeded for a number of reasons. First, he created a brand that had a deliberate, homespun element to it. He was just your old friend running a corner store. Walton helped create the mythology of himself as an all-American success story. It was basically true, but there was more to Sam Walton than apple pie. Positioning the

Wal-Mart brand as home grown and loyally American worked despite the reality that Wal-Mart's success drove smaller stores out of business.

The second element in Walton's success was his ability to create a strong corporate culture. Walton gave people responsibility – "A store within a store" gave departmental heads authority. Then there were profit sharing and incentives. Communication directly from Sam was a corny old technique – the multi-millionaire explaining how much he understood and was concerned about the people on the shop floor – but not many other CEOs put themselves on the line so directly. Again, it was an old trick but it worked.

Third, Wal-Mart invested heavily in information. It shared information with enthusiasm. Wal-Mart even invested in a satellite communications system so learning and experience was quickly communicated within the organization.

For a homely sort of place, Wal-Mart has embraced new technology with fanatical enthusiasm. It was one of the pioneers of EDI. In the late 1980s, Wal-Mart suppliers such as Wrangler and GE were using vendor-managed inventory systems to replenish stocks in Wal-Mart stores and warehouses. Information Technology, such as cash register scanners, means that Wal-Mart is able to obtain a detailed understanding of customers' habits and preferences. This information is then fed to suppliers who are told what to produce, in what quantities and where to ship it. Warehousing and inventory is greatly reduced as a result. This allows the company to use 10 percent of its available space for storage compared to the 25 percent average of its competitors. "Every cost, every time is carefully analyzed, enabling better merchandising decisions to be made on a daily basis," says Randy Mott, senior vice president in charge of information systems.[2]

Wal-Mart is now using data mining software to detect patterns at its 2400 US stores. The aim, according to Rob Fusillo, director of replenishment systems, is to manage inventories "one store at a time, like [each store] was its own dedicated chain."[3] In fact, Wal-Mart possesses the world's largest data warehouse containing a massive 24 terabytes of data.

The process of information gathering begins at the point of sale. Wal-Mart captures point-of-sale transaction information from each of its outlets and moves it through its network to its data warehouse at HQ in Bentonville, Arkansas. The information is then queried if necessary and sales trends analyzed by item and by store. This enables the company to make decisions about replenishment, customer buying trends, seasonal buying trends. The aim is to get the right products to the right store at the right time. "Our business strategy depends on detailed data at every level," says Randy Mott. "Every cost, every line item is carefully analyzed enabling better merchandising decisions to be made on a daily basis."

The final element in Wal-Mart's success is that it has changed its basic formula but only gradually and with great care. The brand has been extended, but only cautiously. The first Sam's Club opened in Midwest City, Oklahoma in 1983; the first Supercenter in 1988; and the first international store in 1991.

Wal-Mart keeps on growing. Its desire to improve is also one of its unique characteristics. In 1977 Walton declared that he wanted to become a $1 billion company within four years; in 1990 the company declared its aim of doubling the number of stores and increasing sales volume per square foot by 60 percent by 2000. Wal-Mart talks big and then delivers. During 1999 it anticipates 40 new discount stores, 150 new Supercenters, 10–15 Sam's Clubs and 75–80 new operations outside the US.

Notes

1   Walton, Sam, *Sam Walton: Made in America*, Doubleday, New York, 1992.
2   Taylor, Paul, "Making close links with shoppers," *Financial Times*, March 17, 1998.
3   Stedman, Craig, "Wal-Mart mines for forecasts," *Computer World*, May 26, 1997.

If there is one company that can manage its brand and chew gum at the same time it's Wrigley's. William Wrigley Jr started by selling soap, then baking powder before he settled on the product that will always be associated with his name, chewing gum.

Wrigley was a pioneer of the use of advertising to promote the sale of branded goods. From the beginning, he realized that commodity products such as soap, baking powder and chewing gum need something to differentiate them in the eyes of consumers. He anticipated the rise of branding in the twentieth century, and to this day the company he founded remains one of its greatest exponents.

His story is one of persistence and opportunism that epitomizes the American entrepreneurial spirit. The brand that he created has stood the test of time. Wrigley's chewing gum remains the best known product in its market.

Today, Wrigley's and its associated companies continue to manufacture just one consumer product – quality chewing gum. In the US, the brands are Wrigley's Spearmint, Doublemint, Juicy Fruit, Big Red and Winterfresh gum; Extra sugarfree gum and Freedent non-tack gum. Additional brands that are produced and marketed outside of America include PK, Orbit and Excell.

Throughout its hundred plus year history, the company has been led by members of the Wrigley family – most of them named William. To date, they go back three generations, starting with the company's founder William Wrigley Jr, who was followed by his son Philip K. Wrigley, whose son William Wrigley is the current president and CEO. Waiting in the wings is Vice president, William Wrigley Jr, who represents the fourth generation.

Gum law

In 1891, William Wrigley moved from Philadelphia to Chicago, where the company's headquarters are located today at the Wrigley Building at 410 North Michigan Avenue. He was 29 years old and had just $32 to his name. His pockets may have been empty but his head was full of dreams. A natural salesman, Wrigley dreamed of starting his own business.

In Chicago he set up a business selling soap to the wholesale trade. Ahead of his time, Wrigley understood the benefits of free promotions. To make his products more attractive to buyers he offered gifts including free baking powder. The baking powder proved more popular than the soap, so like any good entrepreneur, Wrigley moved out of the soap business and into baking powder.

And so it might have continued had it not have been for another of his free promotions. In 1892, he decided to offer two packs of chewing gum with each can of baking powder. It was an even bigger hit than the free baking powder had been. Once again, Wrigley switched businesses. Chewing gum, he felt, was where his future lay. This time he was right.

The first Wrigley chewing gums, Lotta Gum and Vassar, were launched that same year. They were followed in 1893, by Juicy Fruit and Wrigley's Spearmint. The two flavors have been with us ever since.

Wrigley's natural gift for marketing played an important role in the development of the business. He was one of the first entrepreneurs to appreciate the power of branding. To begin with, he concentrated his efforts on his Spearmint gum, advertising it in newspapers. By 1907 he was ready to expand his advertising efforts, but his plans coincided with an economic downturn that hit the Chicago business community. While other companies cut back on their advertising, Wrigley did the opposite. He saw this as the ideal time to get extra attention for his business by advertising. He stepped up his branding efforts and increased production.

Wrigley might have bitten off more than even he could chew, but his counter-cyclical logic, a characteristic of many great entrepreneurs, stood him in good stead. By 1911, Wrigley's Spearmint was America's number one chewing gum. By that time, Wrigley was ready to spread his wings. He introduced PK chewing gum – which was sold in a tightly packed pellet form rather than loose in a box. The name, evidently, was inspired by the advertising slogan that accompanied it: "Packed Tight – Kept Right."

By the time World War I started, Wrigley's was expanding overseas. In 1915, the company established its first factory in Australia, and by 1927 the famous gum went into production in the UK.

The company became a public corporation in 1919. Its stock was first listed on the New York Stock Exchange and the Midwest Stock Exchange in 1923. World War II gave the business received a boost as the allied armed forces purchased large quantities of chewing gum, which was believed to ease the tension, promote alertness and improve morale generally. In 1944, Wrigley's entire production was turned over to the US Armed Forces overseas and at sea (as was the production of Hershey chocolate). It may have lost some of its magic today, but the slogan "Got any gum, chum?" was a big hit with military personnel at the time.

After the war, the invention of a new consumer segment – the teenager – gave Wrigley's another huge boost. When they weren't puffing on a cigarette, rock 'n' roll rebels chewed gum. Its popularity was guaranteed by parents who despised the constant jaw motion of their surly offspring, and branded chewing gum a disgusting habit. This simply made Wrigley's product more popular than ever with high school kids.

As the century advanced and American consumers became ever more hygiene conscious, so fresh breath became a serious issue. Once again, Wrigley's rode to the rescue. Chewing gum had the additional benefit of hiding the smell of cigarettes and alcohol – or so millions of teenagers and errant husbands and wives believed.

The years were kind to Wrigley's. It had the good fortune to be in business at a time when American culture was being exported all over the world. The process started by the archetypal gum-chewing GI in World War II, and immortalized by Hollywood, continued throughout the 1960s, 1970s, 1980s and 1990s.

The demand for all things American, meant that in countries all over the world domestic chewing gums, like domestic cigarettes, were just no substitute for the genuine article. The mass marketing of Americana was and is a triumph of branding.

The irony is that many of those American branded products are no longer made there. Today, Wrigley's produces its distinctively packaged chewing gum in 13 factories around the world: three in North America; four in Europe; one in Africa; and five in the Asia–Pacific region, with a new factory in Russia on its way.

X erox Corporation is one of the great technology brands. Like Hoover, it is a heritage brand. So completely is the name linked with what its product that it has passed into colloquial speech. In Xerox's case, the company took its name from the process it was built on – xerographic copying technology. Americans still talk about "Xeroxing" when they copy a document.

For much of the twentieth century the company has been a dominant and innovative force in some of the fastest changing markets in the world. Today, Xerox competes not just with the other leading photocopier companies but with a growing number of hi-tech digital imaging businesses.

Throughout its sometimes troubled history, it has demonstrated a remarkable ability to keep its brand image contemporary.

Xerox has shown that it has staying power. In the 1970s, the company reinvented itself to fight of the threat from the Japanese. More recently, in the early 1990s, it successfully re-branded itself, repositioning itself from being an old fashioned office equipment supplier to the "document company."

Start copying

Chester Carlson, inventor of the xerographic process, was born in Seattle in 1906. In that same year, the Haloid Company was founded in Rochester, New York, to manufacture and sell photographic paper. The company shared its home town with another aspiring photographic company, Kodak, founded by the entrepreneur George Eastman.

In 1938, Carlson produced the first xerographic image in his laboratory in Queens in New York City. In 1947 the Haloid Company acquired the license to basic xerographic patents taken out by Carlson from Battelle Development Corporation of Columbus, Ohio. A year later, the two companies announced the development of xerography, and the words "Xerox" and "xerography" were patented.

In 1949, the first xerographic copier, the Model A, was introduced. In 1958, Rank Xerox Limited was formed in the UK from a joint venture between the Haloid Company and the Rank Organization. The same year, the Haloid Company changed its name to Haloid Xerox Inc.

In 1959, the revolutionary Xerox 914, the first automatic plain-paper copier, was launched. Office culture would never be the same again. Shortly after its launch in 1959, *Fortune* magazine pronounced the Xerox 914 "the most successful product ever marketed in America." The following year, Haloid Xerox bought all worldwide patents on xerography from Battelle

In 1961, the company was renamed the Xerox Corporation, and was listed on the New York Stock Exchange. A year later Fuji Xerox was launched, and in 1969 Xerox acquired a majority share of Rank Xerox, the European operation.

To many at that time, the company epitomized progressive management thinking. The famous Xerox Palo Alto Research Center (Xerox PARC) in California was set up a year later in 1970 and has been a powerhouse in technological innovation ever since. In 1974, the company was one of the first to establish its own corporate university – Xerox International Center for Training and Development, in Leesburg, VA (renamed Xerox Document University in 1993)

In those heady days the company that held the license to the Xerox technology had the market sewn up. That company was Xerox. But all that was about to change.

In the mid-1970s Xerox was obsessed with competition from Rochester neighbor Kodak – and vice versa. At that time, Kodak had just launched some new high-price copiers, which were seen by Xerox as a direct assault on its market. Distracted by the old foe, the people at Xerox didn't pay too much attention to some upstart companies such as Savin and Canon that were attacking it in small market segments.

All of a sudden, or so it seemed, it could no longer afford to ignore them. These small companies had grown up to become serious rivals. By the time Xerox realized the seriousness of the threat, it had already lost more than half its market share.

By the late 1970s, Xerox, the pioneer of xerography, found itself plunged into a desperate game of catch-up. The company dug in and started an epic comeback. In the battle ahead, the strength of its brand – combined with the Japanese production miracle Total Quality Management – would play an important role. The company installed itself in new headquarters in Stamford, CT, and began to re-invent itself.

While other parts of corporate America clung to the notion that the Japanese success was based not on superior process management but cheap labor costs, Xerox took a long hard look. Its partnership with Fuji made it easier to get a close up view of the Japanese economic miracle. What Xerox quickly realized was that there was more to the superior Japanese performance than the US wanted to admit. Xerox was one of the first American companies to embrace the new Japanese management techniques that had inflicted the damage.

The company became an enthusiastic convert to the Quality movement and set about introducing the "right first time" philosophy into everything it did. In a matter of a few short years, Xerox was back. In 1983, "Leadership Through Quality," the Xerox total quality process, was unveiled. Important lessons had been learned. The company vowed it would never allow complacency to blind it again, or cease in its efforts to remain at the forefront of the technological revolution. A key part of its strategy remained the use of joint ventures and other risk sharing – and knowledge sharing – partnerships.

In the 1980s and 1990s, Xerox was involved in partnerships with most of America's leading technology firms, including Apple, Microsoft and Sun Micro Systems. Its innovative research facility

Xerox PARC is renowned as a hot house for technology break-throughs. Several Silicon Valley successes have been based either on ideas incubated there or heavily influenced by the work carried out there.

This bodes well for the Xerox brand. If there is a single lesson that all technology brands must learn it is that they cannot afford to rest on their laurels even for one second. Innovate or die, is the stark reality. Xerox has shown that it can master new paradigms.

*Y*amaha

I f you ever want to defend a decision to extend a brand cite Yamaha. Yamaha is the best extended brand anywhere. Think of it.

Yamaha makes musical instruments. Quality is not likely to be a problem if you buy a Yamaha organ or any of its guitar and synthesizer products, or its other band or orchestral instruments.

Yamaha makes cars and motor bikes. The Yamaha Motor Corporation began life in 1955 and is now the second largest maker of motor bikes in the world.

All things; most men

Music was the company's first love. In 1887 Torakusu Yamaha (1851–1916) built his first organ and, ten years later, set up Nippon Gakki Company (Japan Musical Instrument Company) with himself as president. The company began producing pianos – upright and then grand pianos – and organs. It won prizes at the St Louis World's Fair in 1904.

It was not until 1953 that its horizons broadened. It was then that the company president, Genichi Kawakami, made his first overseas inspection trip. At this point, Yamaha entered the real hurly burly of industrial competition. It did so with some gusto. In 1954 the company developed a hi-fi player, launched the Yamaha Music School system and also, somewhat bizarrely, began producing its 125 motor cycles. (The company's interest in motor cycle production was, as you would expect, simply one of those quirky things: in the post-war years the company president, Gen-ichi Kawakami, decided to make use of the old production machinery he had by setting up a motor cycle production line. It took a few years to sort the line out and develop the company's first model – understandable as it usually made pianos and organs.)

Yamaha's amazing capacity to stretch its brand into completely unrelated areas has been in evidence throughout. In 1955 it established the Yamaha Motor Company. Its next moves were into archery equipment, a new type of electronic organ and the development and marketing of FRP skis. This was capped brilliantly in 1964 when the company began producing bathtubs. Trumpets, guitars and drums inevitably followed.

During the 1970s the same sort of random pattern emerged. The company moved into tennis rackets, opened a golf course and developed resorts in Japan. The 1980s saw Yamaha develop a carbon composite golf club, begin production of industrial robots and to market ski boots.

The link between these diverse activities is the Yamaha name. The brand is strong enough to carry weight in whatever market Yamaha chooses to enter. The downside of this, of course, is that the company must always get it right.

It is an approach that Virgin chief Richard Branson has admired. Indeed, Branson is critical of the traditional Western view of branding. He likens Virgin's approach to that of some Japanese companies. Referring to the decision by Mars not to use its famous brand name on pet food products, he says: "What I call 'Mars Syndrome' infects every marketing department and advertising agency in the country. They think that brands only relate to products and that there is a limited amount of stretch that is possible. They seem to have forgotten that no-one has a problem playing a Yamaha piano, having ridden a Yamaha motorbike that day, or listening to a Mitsubishi stereo in a Mitsubishi car, driving past a Mitsubishi bank."

Explaining its rationale, Yamaha says that its "very basic corporate objective is reflected in everything that it does, which is to contribute to the enrichment of the quality of lives for people around the world." Grandiose, perhaps, but given the company's prolific range of interests – and its success in virtually all – not one which can be easily dismissed.

Index